Bt $4.37

YALE STUDIES IN ENGLISH

Benjamin Christie Nangle, Editor

VOLUME 150

TWAIN *and the* IMAGE OF HISTORY

by Roger B. Salomon

NEW HAVEN
YALE UNIVERSITY PRESS
1961

 First published in
1961 by Yale University Press, Inc.
Set in Baskerville type and
printed in the United States of America
by Vail-Ballou Press, Inc., Binghamton, N.Y.

Library of Congress catalog card number: 61-6309

This book is published with aid from the foundation
established in memory of Philip Hamilton McMillan
of the class of 1894, Yale College.

FOR PETER

He made history vivid and
meaningful to a new generation

ACKNOWLEDGMENTS

This book had its rude beginnings as a dissertation under Henry Nash Smith at the University of California. As teacher, long-suffering and patient adviser, and friend, he has had an influence on my mind that is beyond adequate acknowledgment. In its various metamorphoses the manuscript was read by Charles Feidelson, R. W. B. Lewis, Benjamin Nangle, and Norman Pearson; their criticisms unfailingly were as constructive as they were honest and perceptive. For such help and encouragement I am deeply grateful. I am equally indebted to David Horne of the Yale University Press for valuable editorial assistance and to Fred Anderson, who, for two long years, was a tireless and expert guide to the Mark Twain Papers.

For permission to quote from certain unpublished materials in the Mark Twain Papers, University of California, I am grateful to Henry Nash Smith, Thomas G. Chamberlain, and The Mark Twain Company. For permission to quote copyright materials, the following acknowledgments are made: Harper and Brothers for *The Mysterious Stranger;* Macmillan, A. P. Watt and Sons, and Mrs. Yeats for W. B. Yeats, "Nineteen Hundred and Nineteen," in *Collected Poems,* 1949; Houghton Mifflin for Archibald MacLeish, "You, Andrew Marvell," in *Collected Poems 1917–1952;* the Grabhorn Press for *Letters from the Sandwich Islands Written for the Sacramento*

Union; and Harcourt, Brace and Faber and Faber for T. S. Eliot, *Murder in the Cathedral.* The chapter on Joan of Arc has been published in an abbreviated form by *The Philological Quarterly,* and the editors have given permission for its inclusion here.

R.B.S.

New Haven, Connecticut
December 1960

CONTENTS

Part One

THE MEANING OF HISTORY

1.

HISTORY AND THE AMERICAN WRITER

> John [Briggs] said, "Can you point out the place where Bear Creek used to be before the railroad came?"
>
> I said "Yes, it ran yonder."
>
> Twain, "Sixty-Seventh Birthday Speech"

> The other world beyond this, which was longed for by the devout before Columbus' time, was found in the new; and the deep-sea-lead that first struck these soundings, brought up the soil of Earth's Paradise. Not a Paradise then, or now; but to be made so, at God's good pleasure, and in the fullness and mellowness of time. The seed is sown, and the harvest must come.
>
> Melville, *Redburn*

> All human affairs are subject to organic disorder.
>
> Melville, *Israel Potter*

In his preface to *The Heidenmauer* James Fenimore Cooper tells of a trip he had taken the year before through the Harz Mountains of central Germany. At one point, a series of ruins dating from pre-Roman, Roman, and medieval times cause him to stop and climb a neighboring mountain (the Teufelstein) from which he can view them better. Under the stimulus of such a setting, a vision of the course of human history passes before his mind's eye: the "furious superstition and debased ignorance" of the barbarian; the ambitions of the ingenious, but sordid Romans; the conflict between monk and baron, both "prey of those incessant and unwearied enemies of the race, the greedy passions." At last, on the ruins of time, he superimposes the dream of America, free, "unenthralled by habits and laws of selfish origin," full of promise for the future—the late and mysterious gift of Providence to agonized mankind.[1]

At once hopeful and pessimistic, Cooper's vision is a paradigm of the response of the American writer to history. Committed by bonds of nationality and culture to the doctrine of historical progress, he has been, at the same time, deeply sensitive to the dark and inert depths of unregenerate man, to the "organic disorder" at the heart of human action. In the work of Mark Twain the potential dilemmas involved in this dualistic response can be observed in their most acute manifestations. Twain's images of history reflect the interaction of a writer's private insights with a major facet of his cultural tradition, an interaction that was to have a radical influence on the form and content of most of his work. Occasionally (as in parts of *Huckleberry Finn*) public and private vision coalesce. More often, behind the ambiguity, the divided intentions, the stylistic lapses of even his best books lies a confused and bitter conflict between his conception of history and his conception of human nature; behind them also lies a passionate desire to escape the moral and aesthetic implications of both through some sort of transcendent dream. When his pessimism deepened late in life, he reformulated his conception of history and groped toward a theory of cycles. On the one hand, his speculations and the literary problems that followed hard on their wake have strong roots in the American past and a distinct relation to those of such diverse contemporaries as James, George, Bellamy,

1. *The Heidenmauer or The Benedictines* (New York, 1872), pp. v–xxxi.

Parkman, and the Adamses (to name only a few). On the other hand, they anticipate in their general drift the twentieth-century revaluation of history which has had such profound repercussions on contemporary literature. This book, in brief, is a closely detailed examination of an important cultural problem at the exact point where it impinges on the art of one major writer. Before describing in some detail the nature of Twain's images of history and analyzing their impact on his work, however, it is important for us to investigate more closely some of the ramifications of the cultural tradition behind these images, in order to understand the limits within which Twain's imagination was to move.

For the nineteenth- and twentieth-century writer in America and England and on the Continent history has served as both a source of aesthetic values and a rationale for political action. At least since the eighteenth century (or whatever earlier date one arbitrarily chooses from which to trace the origins of our modern scientific and industrial world-order) the times have been out of joint and the concept of change has become a kind of First Principle. We have been ceaselessly engaged, as Carl Becker has noted, in either reviling our ancestors or dressing them up, "as models suitable for us to imitate, in shining virtues which in fact they never possessed, which they would perhaps not have recognized as virtues at all." [2] The breakdown of neoclassical theories of art (stressing, as they did, absolute standards) and the concurrent breakdown of the social order under the impact of the French Revolution and burgeoning industrialism found writers seeking to assess the age in which they lived in terms of both the feudal society they sensed to be vanishing and the rational, futur-

2. *The Heavenly City of the Eighteenth Century Philosophers* (New Haven, Yale Univ. Press, 1932), p. 89.

istic ideal of the Enlightenment—an ideal itself heavily compromised by the Reign of Terror and the harsh earlier years of modern capitalism.[3] In the nineteenth century, moreover, the fantastic transformations that people noted everywhere about them in the physical world did much to impress the concept of change dramatically on the thought of the period; steam power (with its adjunct, electricity) became as pervasive and ambiguous a symbol for the age as atomic energy is for our own. Kathleen Tillotson, for example, has described the traumatic effect of the railroad mania after 1845 on English novelists of that time. "Cut off abruptly from the stagecoach world of their youth," she says, "they prolonged and idealized it in memory"; they were haunted by a sense of "betrayal," of division, of "belonging to two ages." [4] It was, of course, the same steam power that drove the trains past Walden Pond and the first Cunard liners into Boston harbor. Henry Adams, a boy of six in 1844, wrote in later years that with the opening of the Boston and Albany Railroad and the coming of the Cunarders "he and his eighteenth-century trog-

3. See Herbert Butterfield, *Man and His Past* (Cambridge Univ. Press, 1955), pp. 17–18: "In the whole general phenomenon of Romanticism we can in fact watch human beings coming to fresh terms with their past after the shock of the French Revolution. At this point the history of historiography touches more intimately a significant phase of general human experience." In particular Butterfield stresses "the way in which the study of the past came to gain in depth through the development of the right imaginative approach—the cultivation of what we call historical-mindedness."

4. *Novels of the Eighteen-Forties* (Oxford Univ. Press, 1954), pp. 106–7. For the poets see Harvey S. Gross, "The Contrived Corridor: A Study in Modern Poetry and the Meaning of History" (diss., University of Michigan, 1954), p. 1: "After the middle of the last century the poets generally felt that the times were changing faster than man's sensibility and moral fiber could stand. Beneath the theistic gloom of Tennyson and the frantic hopefulness of Browning can be felt the terrible insecurity of living in a dissolving world." For the impact of steam power on the American sensibility see Leo Marx, "The Machine in the Garden," *New England Quarterly, 29* (1956), 30–3.

lodytic Boston were suddenly cut apart"; and he added ironically: "For him alone, the old universe was thrown into the ashheap and a new one created." [5] The historical consciousness comes into being, Collingwood notes, when human beings are made aware of violent changes occurring around them, of a world "where things come to be and cease to be." [6] Adams' interest in history was characteristic of a century desperately attempting to measure and evaluate the changes it was so painfully aware were going on.

Twain's sense of change was akin to that of Adams, and with Twain also it led to an abiding interest in history. Both were of the Civil War generation, a generation for whom the Jeffersonian dream seemed not so much a theoretical ideal as a childhood memory, yet a generation forced to live out its adult life (as Alfred Kazin puts it) in a "new America that was cradled in the Civil War, baptized by the Bessemer process and married too early in life to the Republican party." [7] The same notes of uprootedness (though uprootedness from, in some ways, very different traditions) sounds continually in the writing of both men, and leads to a more positive alienation in their later years. To be sure, the Industrial Revolution had been quietly stealing onto the American scene for many years previous to the war. It had, indeed, already been reflected in a good deal of American writing—more, perhaps, than we are yet fully aware of. Leo Marx, who has investigated the problem most fully, stresses the point that "our literature, virtually from the beginning [i.e. 1815] has embodied the experience of a people crossing the line which sets off the era of machine production from the rest of human history." [8] But indus-

5. *The Education of Henry Adams* (New York, Random House, 1931), p. 5.

6. R. G. Collingwood, *The Idea of History* (Oxford Univ. Press, 1956), pp. 20–1.

7. *On Native Grounds* (New York, Harcourt Brace, 1942), p. 18.

8. "The Machine in the Garden," p. 27.

trialism for the Civil War generation was ushered in with trumpet fanfare and roaring guns. Twain and Warner attempted to describe the resulting social upheaval in *The Gilded Age,* but to interpret it meaningfully, they admitted, was beyond them. "The eight years in America from 1860 to 1868," they wrote, "uprooted institutions that were centuries old, changed the politics of a people, transformed the social life of half the country, and wrought so profoundly upon the entire national character that the influence cannot be measured short of two or three generations." The measuring stick would, of course, be history: "History is never done with inquiring of these years, and summoning witnesses about them, and trying to understand their significance" (5, 176–7).[9]

Simply to describe one's childhood in a pre-Civil War village of the Mississippi Valley was to chronicle the dawn of modern history. "Perhaps it is only fair to explain," Twain and Warner note ironically at one point in their description of these conditions, "that we are writing of a bygone age—some twenty or thirty years ago" (5, 48–9). One's life, in effect, spanned the history of a civilization. Twain would write as an older man in "Book Two" of "Eddypus" (his attempt at a universal history) that he was living "in the noonday glory of the Great Civilization, a witness of its gracious and beautiful and all-daring youth, witness of its middle-time of giant power, sordid splendor and mean ambitions, and witness also of its declining vigor and the first stages of its hopeless retreat before the resistless forces which itself had created and which were to destroy it." [1] Thus Twain, like Adams, came finally to believe

9. Unless otherwise noted, all citations are to *The Works of Mark Twain,* Definitive Edition, New York, Gabriel Wells, 1922–25.

1. Unpub. MS, Paine 42a, p. 2, in the Mark Twain Papers, Univ. of California Library, Berkeley, Cal. (cited as MTP). For another example of the tendency in times of great change to move from autobiography to history see Twain's comment about himself as the supposed editor of

that, just as his birth had occurred at the beginning of a "Great Civilization," so his death would find it just short of the final deluge. Such is the way in which a shocked sense of change can lead ultimately to a philosophy of history; one searches for the meaning of one's own experience and this meaning becomes (all too easily) the meaning of history.

Were these changes indicative of social progress, of degradation, or merely of the endless repetition of certain political and social phenomena? Adams and Twain late in life turned in a minority report, but for most of their contemporaries the evolution of society, like (so many thought) the evolution of nature, was purposive; behind the fact of change was a pattern of social, intellectual, and perhaps moral melioration. Although the idea of progress attracted followers from many camps, the dominant theoretical position was what Herbert Butterfield has called "the Whig interpretation of history." From the Whig point of view, progress was the result of, first, a gradual increase in human knowledge through rational grasp of the "laws of nature" and, secondly and concomitantly, the growth of political liberty. A by-product of the Enlightenment, developed by Condorcet and others as a rebuttal to primitivism and fatalism, the Whig interpretation had an almost immeasurable influence on the thought of England and particularly America during the following century, its widespread appeal resulting in part from its efficacy in allaying present anxieties by casting rigorous moral judgments on the Past.[2]

---

a book recording all the people he had known: "He believed that while he wrote his personal histories, general history would flow in a stream from his pen of necessity" ("Book Two, Eddypus," p. 10; MTP).

2. For the assumptions of the Whig historians and the effect of these assumptions on historiography see Butterfield, *The Whig Interpretation of History* (New York, 1951), p. 111 and passim, and George P. Gooch, *History and Historians in the Nineteenth Century* (London, 1920), esp.

Since Mark Twain for the greater part of his life believed (in the words of Macaulay) that his was "the most enlightened generation of the most enlightened people that ever existed" [3] and since this belief was to fail him, with significant repercussions on his art, it is important for us to note why the Whig interpretation was especially attractive to an American and how, in its application to the American experience, it tended to become subtly changed through the infusion of primitivistic elements.

In theory the idea of progress implies either that there is no real evil or that there is steadily less evil in the world. In actual practice, progressivists have always had the greatest difficulty in establishing a necessary correlation between man's intellectual and material development and an absolute improvement in his moral nature. Even Condorcet, the archpriest of human perfectibility, was honest enough to admit that "the labours of recent ages have done much for the progress of the human mind, but little for the perfection of the human race; that they have done much for the honour of man, something for his liberty, but so far almost nothing for his happiness." He could only end his famous *Sketch* with a testimonial of hope and faith in the future.[4] With Condorcet as with many later writers history assumed the ethical and teleological functions of religion.[5] "God is visible in History," George Bancroft assured his audience in an address before the New York Historical Society in 1854. "Since the progress of the race appears to

---

pp. 290–307 (Hallam and Macaulay), pp. 379–92 (Acton), and pp. 402–24 (The United States).

3. Quoted in Gooch, p. 300. For Twain and the Whig interpretation see below, pp. 25–32.

4. *Sketch for a Historical Picture of the Progress of the Human Mind*, trans. June Barraclough (New York, Noonday Press, 1955), pp. 169, 191–2.

5. A point repeatedly documented by recent scholarship. See especially Ernest L. Tuveson, *Millennium and Utopia: A Study in the Background of the Idea of Progress*, Berkeley, 1949; Karl Löwith, *Meaning in History*, Chicago, 1949; and Becker, *The Heavenly City*.

be the great purpose of Providence, it becomes us all to venerate the future." [6] What made this knowledge even more comforting was the assumption that Bancroft shared with his auditors, namely that to venerate the future was synonymous with venerating America or, conversely, that to cast aside the sinful past in this historical Pilgrim's Progress was to cast aside Europe. Cooper, surrounded by the artifacts of ruined societies in the Harz Mountains, could only reconcile his Christian sense of sin with the idea of progress by projecting the whole problem into the future; he, too, put his faith in the providentially directed destiny of America. Even for many European progressivists, tired of depending on mere hope, America loomed across the horizon as a ready-made Utopia.

Commentators everywhere stressed America's uniqueness, her freedom from all those institutions that the eighteenth-century European was beginning to find so burdensome, her reliance on free men rationally governing themselves in accordance with the laws of nature. As Jefferson put it: "We believed that the complicated organization of kings, nobles, and priests was not the wisest or best to effect the happiness of associated man." [7] Freedom from "complicated organization"—here, if we consider the phrase in all its implications, was the source of America's attraction. A hundred years later, during the whole of which time American society was steadily growing more complex, Edward Bellamy in his novel *Looking Backward* described the life of his own era as still essentially "feudal" and looked forward another hundred years to a period when governmental machinery would be "so logical in its principles and direct and simple in its working that it all but

6. Quoted in Charles A. and Mary R. Beard, *The American Spirit*, Vol. 4 of *The Rise of American Civilization* (New York, Macmillan, 1942), p. 180.

7. Quoted in Beard, pp. 102–3.

runs itself," when, in general, "everything touching the relations of men to one another . . . would be simpler, beyond any comparison, than in . . . [the past]." Toward this millennium created by "a few of the plainest simplest . . . maxims" (which, of course, would make everyone good and happy) America had led the world.[8] Bellamy's theory of history and his conception of the roles of Europe and America are thoroughly Jeffersonian; only the relative times have changed. Henry George's Single Tax and Twain's "Man Factories," not to mention his recurrent idyll of American village society, are other illustrations of this continuing ideal of "simplicity."

Clearly, on one level, this whole conception of the simplicity of the future (and, by extension, America)—a conception which pervades eighteenth-century and finds so many important echoes in nineteenth-century thought—reflects the actual political situation of the era: the gradual breakdown of clerical and monarchical institutions in a society where the nature of the new social forms was not readily apparent. On another level, however, the ideal of simplicity has much wider implications, and it is these implications which have done so much to complicate the meaning of the historical role of America, and, in particular the question of our intellectual relations with Europe—that "old" and romantic world that lies within the American mind like a memory of childhood which we alternately seek to embrace and cast away from us.

Actually the exaltation of the American was, for many rationalists, a way out of some of the intellectual dilemmas in which they found themselves. The problem was simply that extreme rationalism had a tendency to verge over into primitivism. Natural laws—eternal, immutable, universal, few in number, easy to comprehend—could be (at least

8. *Looking Backward* (New York, Random House, 1951), pp. 112, 147, 169.

potentially) known by everybody because of certain innate rational instincts. Existing institutions were clearly bad because (in Jefferson's words) they "vitiated and debased" these instincts. Granted this to be true, what kind of institutions were needed to *foster* qualities that were innate in human nature? Plainly those that were themselves rational, simple, immutable, and, above all, few in number. What men required was liberty—freedom to govern themselves.

On the other hand, eighteenth-century writers were also aware of the manner in which civilization had progressed from forest to field to city—in a word, to increasingly *complex* units of organization with their inevitable concomitants of refinement, sophistication, and luxury. But how could this theory of history be reconciled with their rationalistic postulates? As Lois Whitney has pointed out, many of the more popular writers tried to have things both ways: they believed in unlimited progress toward perfection and yet warned against many of the implications of progress. What actually happened is that their theory of history shifted as they searched for a compromise. Whitney, for example, quotes Richard Price as writing: "The happiest state of man is the middle state between the *savage* and the *refined* or between the wild and the luxurious state. Such is the state of society in Connecticut, and some other parts of the American provinces." [9] Price's social ideal appears to be essentially that of Jefferson: neither the barbarian nor the city dweller (proletarian or aristocrat) but the educated small landowner or the independent laborer or craftsman. Cooper defines the "middle state" as that

9. *Primitivism and the Idea of Progress in English Popular Literature of the 18th Century* (Baltimore, Johns Hopkins, 1934), pp. 8–38, 223. In my remarks I am deeply in debt to Whitney's own exhaustive examination of the problem of primitivism and progress. Other important discussions of the problem are Tuveson, p. 179 and passim, and R. V. Sampson, *Progress in the Age of Reason* (Cambridge, Mass., 1956), pp. 67–94.

"between extreme cultivation and ignorance; between the fastidious and sickly perversion of overindulgence, and the selfishness that is the fruit of constant appeals to exertion." [1] For Twain it would be the state of "having only riches enough to be able to gratify reasonable desires, and yet make their gratification always a novelty and a pleasure" (5, 210–11). More extreme primitivists felt that society should move backward to an even lower stage in order to achieve that direct communion with nature so important for the discovery of nature's laws. In any case, progress was seen as a return to a simpler society without a corresponding intellectual retrogression. History was actually going to repeat itself, but with variations according to the degree of one's primitivism. Lovejoy, in his introduction to Whitney (p. xii), notes that primitivism is consistent with degradational theories of history as well as with those that are cyclic or that view progress as a return to a simpler state. We shall have abundant occasion in the work of Twain to note how easy it was to move from one of these theories to another.

Waiting for history to repeat itself or, to put it more concretely, waiting for landed estates to turn back into tidy farms or forests (whichever one prefers) can be discouraging business. Only in America, because of its geographical setting and its providential discovery so late in history could one possess, like Crèvecoeur (or like Natty Bumppo), a fully developed eighteenth-century sensibility and yet actually live a humble and simple life. Here, says Crèvecoeur, the observer might "contemplate the very beginnings and outlines of human society . . . Here we have in some measure regained the ancient dignity of our species; our laws are simple and just, we are a race of cul-

1. *The Heidenmauer,* p. 82. For a superb analysis of the political history in America of the image of the "middle state" see Marvin Meyers, *The Jacksonian Persuasion,* New York, 1960.

tivators, our cultivation is unrestrained, and therefore everything is prosperous and flourishing."[2] The American, new in his oldness, was ideal man: educated, cultured, living a life of reason and yet, most important, always in direct communion with nature and nature's laws. America, as Paine noted in *The Rights of Man,* was not simply the only spot in the political world where the principles of universal reformation could begin; it was also best in the natural world. "In such a situation man becomes what he ought to be."[3] The American, in short, was Adam reborn, the sire of a race of men beginning anew, though perhaps better prepared this time to resist corruption because of the increase in rational knowledge since the time of the first Adam. America represented the ultimate stage of human history, different in kind as well as degree from the rest of civilization, free forever of the suffering, sin, and death so characteristic of the Old World.[4]

Such a thesis in all its various manifestations (it is here presented in its most extreme form) has presented the American writer with a difficult problem. To deny progress was to deny the "manifest destiny"—religious as well as political—of one's country; it was treasonous if not heretical. We shall have occasion to note how time and again Mark Twain's most ringing pronouncements concerning the progress of society were called forth as a patriotic response to threats from abroad: the comments of "Europeanized" American tourists; Walter Scott's "invasion" of the South; the barbs of Matthew Arnold and Paul Bourget. At the same time, Twain, like Melville, Hawthorne, and many others, was equally American in his Calvinistic background, his early and enduring saturation in the realities of sin

2. *Letters from an American Farmer* (London, 1912), p. 12.

3. Quoted in Beard, p. 109.

4. R. W. B. Lewis, *The American Adam* (Chicago, 1955) offers the most illuminating treatment of the influence of the "Adamic idea" on early American writing.

and guilt. One senses more than metaphor in his famous injunctions against the "damned human race." Later observation and experience, in effect, would only reinforce childhood training, but it would bring this training into sharp conflict with historical vision, particularly when this vision was so little able to accept even the *complexity* of civilized man—whatever his ultimate fate.

For the American writer only one other problem has been of comparable importance: Utopia was aesthetically unsatisfying. During his trip up the Rhine toward the Harz Mountains, Cooper had noted that "time is wanting to mellow the view of our historical sites," which still lack "the indefinable colors of distance and convention." [5] Aesthetically, a past was clearly necessary in order to furnish natural objects with the colorful associations so dear to the Romantic mind, but America was a land of the present and the changeless future, a land that had annulled history and cast aside the past as corrupt and immoral. In this impossible dilemma great numbers of writers turned to describing Middlewestern prairies fancifully as English deer parks and rock formations as fairy castles.[6] Such a solution was far from satisfactory. Washington Irving, for example, who was himself to try heroically in later life to describe Oklahoma picturesquely (after having imported German folk tales into the Hudson Valley), escaped to Europe and admitted to readers of his *Sketchbook* that "Europe held forth the charms of storied and poetical association . . . My native country was full of youthful promise: Europe was rich in the accumulated treasures of age. Her very ruins told the history of times gone by, and every mouldering stone was a chronicle. I longed to tread, as it were, in the

5. *The Heidenmauer,* p. ix.

6. For an exhaustive analysis of this problem see Henry N. Smith, "American Emotional and Imaginative Attitudes toward the Great Plains and Rocky Mountains, 1803–1850," diss., Harvard Univ., 1940.

footsteps of antiquity . . . to escape . . . from the common-place realities of the present and lose myself among the shadowy grandeurs of the past." [7] We have already noted how nineteenth-century English novelists from Scott on (and particularly toward the middle of the century) also rejected the commonplace present and set their stories in the past. As Charlotte Brontë said in her introduction to *Shirley:* "We are going back to the beginning of this century: late years—present years are dusty, sunburnt, hot, arid." [8] For American writers, however, the tensions were more acute because ideological lines were more tightly drawn. Europe, Irving says in so many words (and American writers were to repeat endlessly after him), is decadent ("age," "ruins," "mouldering stone") but emotionally compelling ("I longed to tread") and aesthetically satisfying ("charms of storied and poetical associations"); America was the land of the future ("full of youthful promise") but at the present moment it was dreadfully dull.

In Mark Twain, so different an artist in many ways from Irving, we shall note this same dichotomizing of values, but, by the time of Twain's maturity the American writer had an additional past with which to contend: not only of Europe but the more recent past of America itself. Fortunately or unfortunately according to one's point of view, time had refused to stand still in Eden. By the end of Jefferson's administration the rural idyll was perishing, and America was confronted with the same dynamic growth and change (in perhaps even more dramatic proportions) that characterized almost every Western nation during the nineteenth century. Faced with the trauma of the Civil War, the moral breakdown of the Gilded Age, and, in general, the increasingly complex problems of an industrial society, the American writer sensed that the native ideal of enlightened

7. *Works* (New York, 1881), *9*, 14–15.
8. Quoted in Tillotson, *Novels of the Eighteen-Forties,* p. 94.

simplicity was disappearing. Eden was no longer of the present but either a dim future hope (e.g. the growth of the Utopian novel after 1880) or, more important, a nostalgic memory of one's youth. Pre-Civil War village society came to symbolize a peculiarly American past—a past, in this case, with a moral dimension that seemed missing from the present. But both the past of Europe and that of America possessed an aesthetic attraction denied to contemporary life. Americans in search of beauty could either join the exodus to Europe (an exodus whose numbers have never ceased to swell) or seek satisfaction—ironically—in picturesque descriptions of Washington Irving's America. In the course of his career Twain would explore each of these alternatives.

The eighteenth and nineteenth centuries were fascinated with the origins and growth of civilizations; the twentieth is almost obsessed with their decline. To the eighteenth and nineteenth, the growth of rational knowledge was the central cause of progress; to certain thinkers of more recent times it is the surest indication of the seriousness of our historical decline. For Brooks Adams, reason followed the money market; it was antithetical to the imaginative and emotional impulses of decentralized societies. For Henry, its manifestation in modern science would result in the rapid exhaustion of physical energy and thus bring about early world death. Max Nordau believed that frenetic mental activity and the effects of new inventions (among other things) were producing actual physiological changes on the modern mind leading to what he called "organic ruin." For Spengler the whole universe was divided into instinctive and intellectualized activities, with the latter always indicative of decline. But it is Joseph Wood Krutch, reflecting the ideas of these men and others but more sympathetic to the claims of the life of reason, who best sums up what he calls "the paradox of humanism" and the dilemma of the modern intellectual in the face of this paradox. Natural and human ends, he argues, are ultimately irreconcilable because the pursuit of human ends leads to the intellectualization of life and eventually the paralysis of will—both of which, in their turn, bring about social decay. Thus "there is no choice to be made except that between an antlike stability and an eternal recurrence." [9]

The pressure of events has, of course, tended to reinforce the worst fears of the historical pessimists. Time and again the modern writer has echoed the mood of MacLeish's "You, Andrew Marvell":

> And here face down beneath the sun
> And here upon earth's noonward height
> To feel the always coming on
> The always rising of the night [1]

Gone after 1914 was what George Soule has aptly described as "a naive faith in millennialism." More and more individuals have come to agree with Reinhold Niebuhr that "the increase in human power, which is an indisputable fact of historical development, does not seem to solve any basic human problems. It merely presents them in a larger and larger frame." [2] Many, like Niebuhr, have abandoned any attempt to give history a redemptive value or even structural coherence. Others have returned to earlier theories of history, which stressed not the gradual elimination but the inevitable recurrence of evil. This is the final position Twain was to take in *The Mysterious Stranger.* In moving slowly and reluctantly from the party of hope (however qualified) to the party of despair, he embraced a whole revaluation in modern thought: the gradual fading of visions such as that of Cooper on the Teufelstein.

9. *The Modern Temper: A Study and a Confession* (New York, Harcourt Brace, 1929), pp. 19–38.

1. *Collected Poems: 1917–1952* (Boston, Houghton Mifflin, 1952), p. 50.

2. "The Impact of Protestantism Today," *Atlantic Monthly, 181* (1948), 60.

2.

TWAIN AND THE WHIG HYPOTHESIS

Twain's fascination with history was abiding. In 1909 Paine wrote in his notebook: "I am constantly amazed at his knowledge of history—all history—religious, political, military. He seems to have read everything in the world concerning Rome, France, and England particularly" (*33*, 1533).[1] Old favorites like Suetonius or Carlyle's *French Revolution* were to entertain him till literally the very day of his death. But for Twain history had a more important

1. Paine's comment is not quite the exaggeration that it seems. A fairly complete list of the historians Twain probably read thoroughly or consulted at one time or another would include: Suetonius, Tacitus, Caesar, Sir Walter Ralegh, Hume, Macaulay, Carlyle, Lecky, Buckle, Green, Froude, W. F. P. Napier (*History of the War in the Peninsula*), Samuel Dill (*Roman Society*), Thomas Watson (*The Story of France*), Horatio Brown (*Studies in Venetian History*), W. H. Rule (*History of the Inquisition*), Poultney Bigelow (*History of the German Struggle*), Taine, Guizot, Paul La Croix (*Manners: Customs, the Arts and Dress during the Middle Ages*), Michelet, Prescott, Motley, Parkman, Fiske, A. D. White, Tarbell, Woodrow Wilson, Alexander Brown (*The Genesis of the United States*), and C. C. Coffin (*Old Times in the Colonies*). To this impressive list of historians must be added the memoirs, biographies, autobiographies, and travel literature read by Twain—not counting certain specialized works read in the course of historical research done for specific projects (e.g. *Joan of Arc* and *The Prince and the Pauper*). For a more detailed list of Twain's reading see my chief sources, Harold Aspiz, "Mark Twain's Reading—a Critical Study" (diss., UCLA, 1949) and the catalogue of the Mark Twain Library Auction (April 10, 1951).

function than entertainment: nothing less than (as the Sieur Louis de Conte puts it in *Joan of Arc*) "to furnish serious and important facts that teach" (*18*, 63); and Twain would have agreed with Collingwood that the lesson taught by these facts was "what man has done and thus what man is."[2] This conception of the function of history, like so many of Twain's ideas, betrays its eighteenth-century origins; at that time history took the place of religion as the chief source of knowledge about man's character and his ultimate ends.[3] Even when, in the latter part of his life, Twain was most intent on working out his "laws" of history, his chief concern remained the humanistic one of illustrating how these laws work out concretely in the life of man. "His idea was that to write a minute history of persons, of all grades and callings, is the surest way to convey the intelligible history of the time; that it is not the illustrious only who illustrate history, all grades have a hand in it," says an imaginary individual who is supposedly editing Mark Twain's history of the rise, decline and fall of the American Empire. And he adds what at first seems a contradiction: "He also believed that the sole and only history-makers are circumstance and environment; that these are not within the control of man, but that men are in their control, and are helpless pawns who must move as they command."[4] The focus of Twain's history was to be what happens to the individual, although, paradoxically, the individual had no essential part in determining the pattern and outcome of history. Clearly, even at this late date, Twain's

2. *The Idea of History,* p. 10.

3. A conception perpetuated by the Whig historians. Even the Catholic Lord Acton affirmed the quasi-religious function of history. He could write with confidence in 1895 that "the wisdom of divine rule appears not in the perfection but in the improvement of the world . . . history is the true demonstration of religion" (*Essays on Freedom and Power,* New York, Meridian, 1955, p. 36).

4. "Book Two, Eddypus," p. 10.

interest in human beings was anterior to his interest in the social forces behind the human being.

Always for Twain history was a revelation of our human nature and the specific forces which shape it. Quite logically, the books of history he most enjoyed reading were either memoirs—Saint-Simon, Casanova, Pepys, Greville, the Margravine Wilhelmina, and others; highly colored and personalized narratives such as Carlyle's *French Revolution* and Suetonius; or such massive compilations of the vagaries of human thought and conduct as Lecky's *History of European Morals* and Andrew D. White's *Warfare of Science with Theology*. It is these vagaries that, time and time again, draw from him copious and pungent marginal comments. Indeed one has the feeling when reading his marginalia that the chief source, early and late in life, of Twain's interest in history was as documentation for his conviction of the despicability of the human race. Manners, morals, and customs elicited from him an immediate emotional response. Where Andrew D. White, for example, writes that Church authorities refused Renan Christian burial in a place he most loved, Twain marks the passage heavily and notes in the margin: "Why, the sons of bitches." Again, where White describes how, in the Middle Ages, insane people accused of witchcraft were kept awake night after night (a practice which, of course, aggravated their mental illness), Twain writes: "Unspeakably pitiful." [5] The manner in which one could move from such a detail of social history to a *theory* of history is evident in White's own commentary on this passage. "A great modern authority tells us," he says, "that, although modern civilization tends to increase insanity, the number of lunatics at present is far less than in the ages of faith and in the Reformation period. The treatment of the 'possessed,' as we find it laid

5. *A History of the Warfare of Science with Theology in Christendom* (New York, 1901), pp. 119, 362; MTP.

down . . . by orthodox churchmen and jurists, accounts for this abundantly." Comparison of customs is at work and from comparisons emerges a theory of moral progress. Twain's mind normally moved in the same direction. In another notation to White he comments (where White has described how medieval treatment of the poor pauperized the laboring classes): "Apparently the pulpit has attacked each and every thing that is classifiable under the term 'progress'—and in each and every case has suffered defeat and been obliged (in the words of the song) to 'go way back and set down.' "[6]

Other examples from his reading will perhaps better illustrate the kind of information Twain sought from history and the nature of the revelation presumably offered by this information. His copy of *The Memoirs of the Duke of Saint-Simon* is filled with such notations as "Manners of the Time," or "The Court is a family of cats and dogs who are always quarreling over scraps of offal" or "These low scoundrels, these shams, these play-acting sentimental pukes" after certain descriptions of activities among the French aristocracy. Again, as in the case of White's book, one marginal comment shows that Twain is placing these manners and morals within an historical frame. He scrawls across the top of the page on which Saint-Simon claims that the king's mistress, Madame de Montespan, is a very religious person: "From the year AD 300 to the year 1800 may be described as the age of pious w - - - - s."[7] Sexual promiscuity mingled with piety apparently was characteristic of an historical epoch that allegedly stretched from Constantine's toleration of Christianity to the French Revolution. From a comment on morals, Twain has produced, at least in germ, a theory of history; if we collect and compile the

6. Ibid., p. 287.

7. 3 vols. London, n.d.; MTP. Citations are to *1*, 82, 86; *2*, 117; and *1*, 375, respectively.

vicious manners and morals of the people living in the years 300–1800 we, of course, arrive at the *Connecticut Yankee* and that famous indictment of Catholicism beginning "In two or three little centuries it had converted a nation of men to a nation of worms" (*14*, 64–5).[8]

Indeed, Twain's marginal comments in the work of Saint-Simon, White, and others shed a good deal of light on his own intentions as an historical novelist. Conduct was, to be sure, rigidly determined by institutions, but Twain was less interested in abstract analysis and delineation of these institutions than in pointing out the way they expressed their nature in "laws," that is, in concrete rules prescribing and limiting man's actions and thus creating his morals and manners. The years 300–1800 (to go back to our previous example) were, as he thought, a single, unified epoch whose chief institutions were Catholicism and its bastard offspring feudalism; he accused these institutions of promulgating cruel laws which made people do terrible things to each other. In writing about history it was these terrible things that had to be stressed. He was explicitly describing this kind of history when he noted on the flyleaf of Saint-Simon's *Memoirs* (Vol. 1): "This, and Casanova and Pepys, set in parallel columns, would offer a good coup d'oeil of French and English high life of that epoch."

Such a coup d'oeil was precisely what he set out to create in the *Connecticut Yankee.* He avoided the (to him) less important problems of verisimilitude and anachronism by casting the story in "mythical Arthur's day," which allowed him to introduce laws "not known to have existed in King Arthur's time, of course," but which existed in Christian lands later. The episodes in the book (he wrote, in an unused preface) are "not inventions but . . . drawn from history; not always English history but mainly from that

8. See below, pp. 101–2, for the complete passage.

source." In another preface he is still more explicit; some of the harshest laws he admits having borrowed from pre-Revolutionary France and the southern slave states.[9] At the bottom of almost all his thinking and writing about history lies this process of collecting and collating morals, manners, and customs. Certainly his belief in the moral and material progress of nineteenth-century Western Civilization—a belief which, with many qualifications, was central to his social criticism before 1890—sprang neither from cosmic optimism nor Spencerian theories of evolution, but from a comparative study of human conduct at different times and places. Indeed, Twain always rejected teleological evolution, and this was later to be an influence on his final rejection of the theory of progress. The degree of his faith, even as a young man, in Providence and the beneficence of nature can be seen from a passage in *Roughing It:* "Providence," he wrote, "leaves nothing to go by chance. All things have their uses and their part and proper place in Nature's economy: the ducks eat the flies—the flies eat the worms—the Indians eat all three—the wild cats eat the Indians—the white folks eat the wild cat—and thus all things are lovely" (*3*, 261–2). Only the tone was to change in his later writing.

It remains for us to examine more specifically the particular lessons taught by the comparative examination of human conduct. Between Twain and the Enlightenment stood the Whig historians, for whom history recorded the development of knowledge and political liberty. Lord Acton summed up the theoretical position of an historical movement stretching from Hume, Voltaire, and Condorcet through Hallam and Macaulay, when, in a speech of 1877, he described liberty as the "delicate fruit of a mature civilization" and went on to note:

9. "Two Unused Prefaces to *A Connecticut Yankee,*" Paine 91; MTP.

> scarcely a century has passed since nations, that knew the meaning of the term, resolved to be free. In every age its progress has been beset by its natural enemies, by ignorance and superstition, by lust of conquest and by love of ease, by the strong man's craving for power and the poor man's craving for food. During long intervals it has been utterly arrested, when nations were being rescued from barbarians and from the grasp of strangers . . . If hostile interests have wrought much injury, false ideas have wrought still more; and its advance is recorded in the increase of knowledge, as much as in the improvement of laws.[1]

With Acton's main contention Twain was, of course, in complete agreement, though, significantly, where Acton dated the actual concrete advance of liberty from the American Revolution (i.e. "scarcely a century" from 1877), Twain dated it from the overthrow of the Bourbons. For Acton the American Revolution was in the main stream of English constitutional development, while the French was badly marred by atheism, immorality, and a passion for extreme equality imposed by violence. Twain was anti-Catholic, deeply influenced by Carlyle, and fascinated with violence but generally shared the Whigs' fear of mob rule and extreme democracy. In any case, he noted in an unpublished 1889 preface to the *Yankee:* "Human liberty—for white people—may fairly be said to be one hundred years old this year. What stood for it in any previous century of the world's history cannot rationally be allowed to count." [2] For both men the increase of knowledge and the improvement of laws had led to the steady shift of power away from arbitrary authority and into the hands of the common man.

1. *Essays,* pp. 53–4. For Acton on the relative values of the American and French Revolutions see pp. 106–9.

2. Paine 91; MTP. Occasionally he showed his awareness of the influence of the American on the French Revolution.

Because of the curious mixture of rigid determinism and moral focus that characterized his thinking, it was particularly easy for Twain to make the additional postulation of some sort of improvement in the fundamental nature of man: at least a diminution of organized cruelty and the growth of essential refinement.

The Whig historian, says Herbert Butterfield, loves the past for certain values he cherishes in the present; in other words, he searches for the roots of the present and passes stern judgment on all those who have presumed to hinder the passage of Western society from medieval tyranny to modern liberty.[3] Such was Mark Twain's approach to English history during the years from 1880 to 1890, which constituted the high-water mark of his belief in the "law of human progress, human betterment, otherwise called civilization." In his most complete nonfictional analysis of the development of England, an unpublished manuscript entitled "On Progress, Civilization, Monarchy, etc.," (probably written in the later 1880's) he marks the "clearly defined steps" by which English civilization has progressed from a "sufficiently low level." These "steps" are, in effect, a kind of check list of Whig-Liberal legislation: destruction of English serfage and slavery; loosening of the control of the Church; introduction of representative government and considerable extension of the suffrage; penal reform (reduction of penalties for minor crimes and abolition of restriction of counsel from state prisoners); army reform (abolition of purchase and relinquishment of restrictions of military promotions to high born); abolition of impressment; and the gradual stripping of various privileges from the nobility. All the emphasis is on political and legal rather than economic reform—on the wresting of power from the aristocracy and church in favor of the commonalty and on the growth of equality of justice and privilege.

3. *The Whig Interpretation of History,* pp. 11–13, 95. See above, p. 9.

This was only the *trend* of English history; liberty as an accomplished fact—what Twain calls "Manhood"—was the unique feature of American civilization. Twain's choice of words suggests the eighteenth-century bedrock of much of his thought and also reflects again his constant habit of seeing historical conceptions in human terms. "What I mean by Manhood," he wrote, ". . . is a condition where all roads to betterment are public highways, not free to one and forbidden to another; where equal capacities have an equal chance . . . where a man's origin counts nothing for him and nothing against him; where a man is not a god because he was born in a church, nor a corpse because he was born in a graveyard, but is just a man in both instances —no more, no less." [4] America's social mobility, in short, encompassed and went a step beyond English constitutional liberty. For both countries, however, the future was equally glorious; there was "no limit to human possibilities as regards human betterment. . . . These two civilizations have risen out of primeval night and they rest upon the horizon. Could they stop there if they would—with the zenith inviting them and the law of their inspiring march impelling them to seek it and achieve it?" [5] This is the most optimistic statement regarding the meaning of history that Twain ever wrote and, to my knowledge, the one occasion on which he ever predicted endless and inevitable *future* progress for England and America, although he was, of course, constantly describing the progress made since the Middle Ages. Apparently the law of the growth of human liberty, operating endlessly, made future progress inevitable and limitless.

In Twain's fiction of the period from 1880 to 1890, the

4. Paine 102b, pp. 8, 23–6; MTP. Cf. Acton's cold and chaste definition of liberty: "the assurance that every man shall be protected in doing what he believes his duty against the influence of authority and majorities, custom and opinion" (*Essays*, p. 55).

5. Paine 102b, p. 29.

two great monuments to this belief in political and juridical growth (which, in turn, effect changes in human nature) are *The Prince and the Pauper* and *A Connecticut Yankee.* Both books—and almost every comment Twain ever wrote about both books—lay special emphasis on the development of laws that have enhanced human rights and dignity. As a novelist, however, Twain had a distinct advantage over the Whig historian; where the latter had, perforce, to be content to search out tortuously the "roots" of the present in the past and wait patiently while they grew, Twain was able, on the one hand, to exaggerate these roots in *The Prince and the Pauper* and, on the other, to ignore roots entirely and drag into the past the fully matured plants. Like Defoe, Twain carried the impatience of the Whig historian to its ultimate extreme: to the point of artificially "speeding up" the evolution of modern civilization. He could not wait to set free the naked, unadorned man of enterprise.

What is most significant about Robinson Crusoe and the Yankee is that they are both symbolic of the radical new attitude toward human experience to which the Whig historian, adding to the evidence but following assumptions laid down by eighteenth-century writers, attributed the alleged progress of Western society. Condorcet, as J. B. Bury has noted, insisted on " 'the indissoluble union' between intellectual progress and that of liberty, virtue, and the respect for natural rights, and on the effect of science in the destruction of prejudice." [6] Likewise, for both Macaulay and Acton the Prime Mover of recent history was the growth of knowledge. According to Macaulay, "it is not merely that new principles have been discovered, but that new faculties seem to be exerted. It is not that at one time the human intellect should have made but small progress, and at another time have advanced far; but that at one

6. *The Idea of Progress* (New York, Macmillan, 1932), p. 209.

time it should have been stationary, and, at another time, constantly proceeding." Ancient thought (and medieval as it was dominated by ancient thought) was both static and impractical; it reflected both the parochialism and sense of exclusiveness of the Greeks and their refusal to cultivate natural science "for the purpose of increasing the power and ameliorating the condition of mankind." The modern attitude Macaulay traced to Bacon: "Two words form the key to the Baconian doctrine, Utility and Progress. The ancient philosophy disdained to be useful, and was content to be stationary." [7]

In a significant sketch called "A Majestic Literary Fossil," written in the same year as the publication of *A Connecticut Yankee,* Twain echoed, in part at least, these ideas of Macaulay. In this sketch he attacked the author of an old book of medicine used in his youth for believing in the superior wisdom of Greek and Roman doctors and remarked, in the course of a harrowing description of the medical practices of the early nineteenth century, that "if I were required to guess offhand . . . what is the bottom cause of the amazing material and intellectual advancement of the last fifty years, I should guess it was the modern-born and previously non-existent disposition on the part of men to believe that a new idea can have value." Such acceptance of innovation and indifference to older ideas Twain called "the most sweeping that has ever come over mankind in the history of the race" (*22,* 329–32). Aware of his uniqueness, the Yankee notes that in the Arthurian Kingdom "for a man . . . to have had an idea that his ancestors hadn't had, would have brought him under suspicion of being illegitimate" (*14,* 201). In the figure of the Yankee, Twain was to create, as Defoe had created in Crusoe, innovation incarnate, the practicing empiricist, the Baconian utilitarian and

7. *Critical, Historical and Miscellaneous Essays* (New York, 1860), *1,* 410; *3,* 436, 442. See also *3,* 271–2, 436–64.

progressive, the Whig bourgeois. The Yankee himself is aware of his kinship with Defoe's earlier prototype of modern man. "I saw that I was just another Robinson Crusoe cast away on an uninhabited island," he says, shortly after arriving in Camelot, "with no society but some more or less tame animals, and if I wanted to make life bearable I must do as he did—invent, contrive, create, reorganize things; set brain and hand to work, and keep them busy. Well, that was my line" (*14*, 53). Clearly, modern civilization was indebted to such men for its growth of knowledge and its concurrent advance in the arts of politics and human relations. In this process the role of America was crucial because America offered the most perfect environment for the technician. "She has had unobstructed freedom during 113 years to create, by her inventions and her patent laws, *Modern Civilization*," Twain wrote in a marginal note of 1889. "If she had remained a British appendage it is likely that the bulk of this brilliant material advancement would have been postponed a good while. Ours was the first sane patent law (1794). It started the world's wheels and they are whirling yet." [8] At the height of his historical optimism Twain conceived of material and political progress as going hand in hand toward the same beneficent goal.

Goaded by patriotism, he returned to the same theme as late as 1894 in an unpublished manuscript attacking Paul Bourget. The discovery of America, he pointed out to Bourget, "was the discovery of the mill-site where we were to build the mill from which was to be produced the bulk of the modern civilization." He admitted (in the great tradition of American apologetics) that America had no art "but civilization is another matter. It is a large word and

8. In Charles C. F. Greville, *The Greville Memoirs: A Journal of the Reigns of King George IV and King William IV*, ed. Henry Reeve (London, 1874), *1*, 242; MTP. Italics are Twain's. Twain's comment comes after Greville questions how much, if anything, England lost when the American Colonies won their freedom.

stands for a large thing—in these latter days. A hundred years ago it was a small thing and simple: now it is vast and complex in its makeup." After these introductory remarks he listed a series of political and legal developments and inventions which had made man's life "easier and freer and pleasanter than it was before, and less mean and bitter and hampered": (the order is his) political liberty, religious liberty, reduction of capital penalties, equality before the law, women's rights, application of anaesthesia to surgery, rational patent laws, development of patents, the cotton gin, and, finally, a whole array of mechanical devices which is almost a history of American technology. Far from being denigrated or considered a mere by-product, material progress is claimed as an American discovery and considered as a Prime Mover of modern civilization, on equal terms with political liberty and legal reform.[9]

As we shall observe in later chapters, Twain had strong emotional—and occasionally intellectual—reservations about these theories during the very years he advocated them most vehemently. At best, benevolent historical determinism was only a substitute for a moral and psychological freedom which he could dream about but not rationally locate in human experience. By the end of the 1890's, however, under the impetus of personal tragedy, an increasing sense of guilt, and a larger awareness of the plutocratic and imperialistic drift of American society, Twain had brought the Whig hypothesis itself under direct attack and was moving toward a theory of historical cycles.

9. "Have We Appropriated France's Civilization?" De Voto (cited as DV) 217, pp. 1–35; MTP.

3.

THE MAD PHILOSOPHER:

TWAIN AS PROPHET OF DOOM

In the same notebook entry in which he comments on Twain's knowledge of history, Paine goes on to describe how

> last night we stopped playing billiards while he [Twain] reviewed, in the most vivid and picturesque phrasing, the reasons of Rome's decline. Such a presentation would have enthralled any audience—I could not help feeling a great pity that he had not devoted some of his public effort to work of that sort. No one could have equaled him at it. He concluded with some comments on the possibility of America following Rome's example, though he thought the vote of the people would always, or at least for a long period, prevent imperialism. [*33*, 1533]

Twain's role in this scene is characteristic of his later years; only his guarded optimism seems out of place. More often he was the Cassandra-like "Mad Philosopher," scorned and mocked but relentlessly predicting the imminent doom of his rotten society; or the "Professor of the Science of Historical Forecast" lecturing on the "laws" of history ("Letters from the Earth"); or the "Father of History," who had passed on to posterity the story of the decline and fall of his civilization before being hanged by the new totalitarians ("Eddypus").

Twain wrote of the Mad Philosopher that he "merely builds prognostications, not prophecies . . . builds them out of history and statistics, using the facts of the past to forecast the probabilities of the future. It was merely applied science." [1] The echoes of Buckle (whom he had read) in Twain's references to "laws" and statistical predictions suggest the influence of positivism on his later thought. They suggest also the degree to which he and Henry Adams were caught up in the same historical currents and drifted in the same direction. Both were soaked in the eighteenth-century tradition of didactic and apocalyptic history; both tried to fuse this tradition with nineteenth-century scientific dogmatism (with Twain, at least, this was more a desire than a fulfillment); and both made their most significant attempts only when their early dreams of a democratic world order had changed to despairing fears of world catastrophe. But above all, for both men history was not only prophetic (or capable of scientific prediction), but prophetic of the same things at roughly the same times in their lives.[2] William Jordy's description of the radical reversal in Adams' theory of history could equally well stand for that in Twain's: "From his optimistic belief that democracy afforded the ultimate theme for historical study, Adams

1. "Letters from the Earth," pp. 130–60; MTP. This is the collective title given by De Voto to several manuscripts which he brought together and edited but never published. Page references are to his typescript.

2. *A Connecticut Yankee* (1889) and the *History of the United States during the Administration of Jefferson and Madison* (1889–91) sum up the early historical speculations of the two men. For their later ideas on history cf. Adams' "The Tendency of History" (1894), expanded into *A Letter to American Teachers of History* (1910) and *Mont-Saint-Michel and Chartres* (1904) with Twain's *Joan of Arc* (1895–96), *The Mysterious Stranger* (begun 1897), "Eddypus" (1903), and the historical portions of "Letters from the Earth" (probably 1905–06). Brooks Adams (*The Law of Civilization and Decay,* 1895) also figures significantly in this *fin de siècle* movement toward historical pessimism.

shifted to the pessimistic assertion that annihilation provided the final goal of historical prophecy." [3] Only the details differed; where Adams anticipated world death and embraced the Middle Ages, Twain fell back on cycles and wrote of the return of hated medieval "night."

In both his published and unpublished work we can trace Twain's growing doubts about his earlier assumptions as these doubts develop out of certain potential problems involved in the assumptions themselves. In the first place, he was forced to come to terms with some of the complexities involved in the apparently simple idea of the "growth of knowledge." Science, we are constantly reminded, "is remaking not only the outer world in which we live, but also the inner world of our thoughts and ideals." [4] We ceased to burn witches at the same time that we were inventing the steam engine. The "growth of knowledge," in other words, is a growth in many different directions, but the crucial question remains whether developments in all these various directions are of equal value or even compatible. Not until the end of his life did Twain begin to discriminate consciously when he talked about the growth of knowledge, to become aware, indeed, of the *need* for conscious discrimination.

At the height of Twain's historical optimism there was little or no explicit discrimination between the different directions that the growth of knowledge had taken—only, at most, discriminations at the more or less subconscious level which betray themselves stylistically in terms of structural emphasis and tone. In *A Connecticut Yankee,* to take the most striking example, the Yankee himself, as we have already noted, is completely representative of the politi-

3. *Henry Adams: Scientific Historian* (New Haven, Yale Univ. Press, 1952), p. 128.

4. Edwin G. Conklin, "Science and the Faith of the Modern," in *Great English and American Essays,* ed. Douglass S. Mead (New York, Rinehart, 1956), p. 191.

cally free, technologically advanced society. On one occasion when Twain discussed with a Baltimore group, before whom he was giving a prepublication reading, his conscious purposes in writing the novel, he went out of his way to stress the technological significance of the Yankee. We are struck, he told his audience, with "the utter simplicity, the naked and barren simplicity" of life in the Middle Ages, "a life . . . barren . . . of anything worthy to be called knowledge." He asked them to "conceive of the blank and sterile ignorance of that day, and contrast it with the vast and many-sided knowledge of this. Consider the trivial miracles and wonders wrought by the humbug magicians and enchanters of the old day, and contrast them with the mighty miracles wrought by science in our day of steam and electricity. Take a practical man, thoroughly equipped with the scientific enchantments of our day and set him alongside of Merlin, the head Magician of Arthur's time, and what sort of show would Merlin stand?" [5] Actually, in the finished book, not only are the Yankee's scientific miracles almost as trivial as those of Merlin, but modern technological civilization in general is sharply satirized when it is not shunted into the background and ignored completely. Clearly the historical focus of the novel lies in those other ramifications of the growth of knowledge which Twain grouped so carelessly with technology—in customs and laws which tend to debase or elevate our moral nature.

Of course, as an amateur historian Twain was eager for generalizations and bored with facts—especially those which he felt were self-evident to his contemporaries—and this is perhaps another reason why the details of the Yankee's civilization are so little stressed. In his role of practising humorist, moreover, Twain could seldom resist the topical joke, however irrelevant it might be to his more

5. "A Reading from the *Yankee*," DV 21, pp. 2–3; MTP.

serious concerns.[6] Neither of these reasons, however, fully explains the frequency with which Twain's discussions of technology lapse into satire and burlesque. Even in his answer to Paul Bourget, there creep into his catalogue of mechanical marvels such items as spiritualism, Christian Science, and electrocution.[7] In any case, by 1897 more or less subconscious discriminations were becoming overt and meaningful. "Queen Victoria's Jubilee," a short essay of that year, is still progressivist in theme but shot through with irony and qualifications. These qualifications are first apparent in Twain's familiar description of the last hundred years: "British history is two thousand years old, and yet in a good many ways the world has moved further ahead since the Queen was born than it moved in all the rest of the two thousand put together. A large part of this progress has been moral, but naturally the material part of it is the most striking and easiest to measure." This incipient distinction between moral and material progress is further developed when Twain discusses each—separately. Under "moral progress" (by which Twain means, of course, progress in institutions which will inevitably make men better) is the usual list: legal reform, liberty, free newspapers, workers' rights, women's rights, and modern medicine (specifically "humanitarian" technology is now carefully selected out and credited to "moral progress"). Modern inventions this time remain unenumerated, but Twain remarks that they have "made life . . . easy and difficult, convenient and awkward, happy and horrible, soothing and irritating, grand and trivial, an indispensable blessing and an unimaginable

6. One small but typical example: from an English newspaper of 1885 Twain extracted the advertisement reading "Use Peterson's Prophylactic Tooth-Brush—All the Go," carried by one of the Yankee's reformed knights. See below, pp. 110–11, n. 9, for Twain's own list of sources consulted when writing the *Yankee.*

7. "Have We Appropriated France's Civilization?" p. 35½.

curse" (*29*, 202–3). These inventions are, to say the least, a mixed blessing.

A growing disillusionment with modern society was thus causing Twain to sense the problematic nature of his previously unexamined assumptions about the growth of knowledge. On the one hand, "science" (the rise of empirical philosophy), by freeing the intellect from "Catholic" and "feudal" ideas, had brought about the growth of political and religious liberty and legal and social equality; but what if, on the other hand, "science" (technology, the industrial revolution) was simultaneously destroying simplicity, honesty, and goodness in life by stimulating greed and fostering "money-madness" and a lust for power? What if this greed and lust eventually created a new oligarchic despotism? What if, in other words, the growth of knowledge in one direction was annulled by the growth of knowledge in another so that the end result was not permanent progress but the rise, maturity, and decay of a civilization—so that the end result, in short, was simply a cycle of history? This was, of course, the conclusion to which Twain had come by the time he sat down to write his so-called "Eddypus Cycle," which was to be a history of the rise, decline, and fall of the great American civilization.

First Twain conjures up the familiar image of Jeffersonian America (which he carefully distinguishes from preindustrial European society) "reposing in peace and contentment in the shelter and protection of liberal and wholesome laws honestly administered by men chosen for their proved ability, education, and purity, under Chief Magistrates illustrious for statesmanship, unassailable integrity, and dauntless moral courage." On this "drowsing world" bursts the "Great Civilization" of the nineteenth century, a century "sown thick with mechanical and scientific miracles and wonders . . . that have changed the face of the world." The origin of this "splendid nightmare" world, says Twain, "whether from hell or from heaven is matter for this history to determine." That, in general, he determines the matter negatively is clear from the whole drift of the book. Not only is his history supposedly dug out of a vault at a time ten centuries later when the world has been completely enveloped in a new darkness, but the eclipse of the "Ages of Light" is described as the result of "natural and unavoidable developments of the disease called civilization. Within certain strict bounds and limits civilization was a blessing; but the very forces which had brought it to that point were bound to carry it over the frontier sooner or later and that is what happened. The lamp of its being was progress, advancement, and there was no power that could stop its march, or even slacken its pace. With its own hands, it opened the road and prepared the way for its destroyer." Civilization's destroyer was Christian Science, which Twain envisaged as a new Catholicism sweeping America and the West in general, burning the books, instituting thought-control, and eventually returning society to medieval barbarism.[8] Knowledge had died of "his own too-much"; the cycle of history was complete. The similarity between the underground vault in "Eddypus" and the underground room in *Looking Backward* suggests that Twain may have had Bellamy in the back of his mind.[9] In any case, his "Eddypus Cycle" is a clear

8. "Eddypus, Book One," pp. 4–25 and "Two," pp. 15–39. Again burlesque creeps into Twain's actual description of the scientific revolution. In one of his more revealing jokes he telescopes all the great scientists from Galileo to Edison into the nineteenth century. What Twain wishes to emphasize is merely the exhilaration, the sense of release, furnished by the new scientific discoveries. At the same time, the oversimplifications of the Whig interpretation are mercilessly, if unwittingly, exposed by this naive historian. Twain could no more place Galileo in the context of the sixteenth century than he could place Joan of Arc in the fifteenth (see below, pp. 168–74).

9. Twain had read *Looking Backward* in 1889 and called it "fascinating" (Notebook 24, p. 30; MTP).

(even if not an intentional) rebuttal to Bellamy's optimism and a forerunner of the anti-utopian literature of this century.

By 1900, in short, Twain could no longer embrace all the implications of the "growth of knowledge." He dreamed again the American dream of a society liberal without being complex, politically sophisticated yet socially austere and simple—a society whose passing he had described as a young writer in *The Gilded Age*—and his dreaming heightened an already fierce nostalgia. In the papers of the family of Adam (his other extended fictional account of modern history) the strictures against the later nineteenth century are even more severe. "Our wonderful civilization," says the Mad Philosopher, Reginald Selkirk, rhetorically at one point. "I will not object to the adjective—it rightly describes it—but I do object to the large and complacent admiration which it implies. By all accounts . . . the pure and sweet and ignorant and unsordid civilization of Eden was worth a thousand million of it." He goes on to point out that our civilization is wonderful only "in certain spectacular and meretricious ways; wonderful in scientific marvels . . . in material inflation, which it calls Progress . . . wonderful in its extraordinary financial and commercial achievements . . . in its hunger for money . . . It is a civilization which has destroyed the simplicity and repose of life; replaced its contentment, its poetry, its soft romance-dreams and visions with the money-fever." Selkirk, the "Professor of the Science of Historical Forecast," awaits the inevitable collapse of Adamic society, a collapse to be ushered in this time, apparently, not by Christian Science but by a technician dictator. The latter, in turn, would blow himself up with his own secret weapon after sweeping the continent "from end to end with fire and sword." [1]

1. "Letters from the Earth," pp. 128–37. In my comments I am deeply indebted to De Voto's arrangement of these fragmentary manuscripts and

In such remarks, of course, Twain echoes some of the deepest fears of the American mind. Certainly the stance of the American writer from Cooper to Pound has been that of "looking backward," fearful of degeneration, fearful that the ideal society was already in the past or rapidly disappearing. We have already noted how the seeds of a cyclical theory of history lurked in certain eighteenth-century doctrines of progress—imbued, as they were, with the primitivistic and rationalistic ideal of simplicity.[2] Because it completely mirrored this simplicity, Jeffersonian democracy seemed to fit the theoretical qualifications of the progressivists so perfectly that there was nowhere left for society to go but down. Even a sophisticated historian like Acton found himself in this dilemma when describing the American experience:

> There was a time in the Presidency about fifty-five years ago which men still speak of as "the era of good feeling," when most of the incongruities that had come down from the Stuarts had been reformed, and the motives of later divisions were yet inactive. The causes of old-world trouble, popular ignorance, pauperism, the glaring contrast between sick and poor, religious strife, public debts, standing armies and war,—were almost unknown. No other age or country had solved so successfully the problems that attend the growth of free societies, and time was to bring no further progress.[3]

The Whig historian is here trapped by his own oversimplifications. The suggestion, in this passage, of a development to a supreme point and then some kind of falling off be-

---

his editorial comments. For a discussion of the significant parallels between the dictator and the Yankee see below, p. 123.

2. See above, pp. 12–14.

3. *Essays on Freedom and Power,* p.108.

comes, in more pessimistic hands, a theory of rise and fall —in which case, America loses its uniqueness and steps forward to take its place in the long procession of civilizations that have already risen and fallen. Certainly this is the position Twain had more or less arrived at even before the outbreak of the Spanish-American war.

It was imperialism that destroyed the last vestiges of his belief in American uniqueness. The oppression of weak and ignorant peoples seemed to him conclusive evidence of the way in which later nineteenth-century civilization had corrupted the early ideals of the Republic. As a conqueror America became indistinguishable from other conquering nations and took her place with them in the inexorable historical process that would eventually lead to destruction. In his fictional sketch of American history in "Eddypus" Twain developed these ideas at some length:

> It was the intention of the Americans to erect a stately Democracy in their land, upon the basis of freedom and equality before the law for all; this Democracy was to be the friend of all oppressed people, never their oppressor . . . it was never to crush or betray struggling republics. The Americans required that these noble principles be embodied in their Declaration of Independence and made the rock upon which their government should forever rest. But George Wishington [sic] strenuously objected. He said that such a Declaration could not long survive in purity; that as soon as the Democracy was strong enough it would wipe its feet upon the Declaration and look around for something to steal . . . if it happened to be a republic no matter. . . .
>
> Still the Declaration was put upon the desired plan, and the Republic did really set up fair temple upon the lofty height. Wishington did not live to see his

> prophecy come true, but in time it did come true, and the government henceforth made the sly and treacherous betrayal of weak republics its amusement, and the stealing of their land and the assassination of their liberties its task. This endeared it to the monarchies and despotisms, and admitted it to their society as a world power.[4]

What America's becoming a "World Power" meant to Twain is evident from his comments in a sketch called "History 1000 Years from Now," another of his many abortive attempts late in life at writing fictional history. With heavy irony he imagines that it has been a thousand years "since the happy accident—or series of accidents—occurred which after many years rescued our nation from democracy and gave it the blessed refuge and shelter of a crown." The first of these "accidents," he makes clear, was the seizure of the Philippine Archipelago.[5] With imperialism, in other words, the American nation took the first decisive step down the path of history that would lead back to what Twain loosely called feudalism and monarchy.

Charles and Mary Beard have pointed out that Twain's interpretation of imperialism as a return to Old World barbarism and corruption was shared by (among others) Howells, George D. Herron, Bishop John L. Spalding, and William Graham Sumner. The more common view, on the other hand, was that America's Far Eastern expansion represented the consummation of national and, indeed, world history—the final goal of progress.[6] Other individuals of the time maintained a more idiosyncratic position. Brooks Adams combined jingoism and historical pessimism; Amer-

4. "Book One," pp. 17–18.
5. MS Paine 52b, pp. 2–4; MTP.
6. *The American Spirit,* pp. 582–91. Twain ridicules the optimistic historical interpretation of imperialism in "The Fable of the Yellow Terror," DV 359a; MTP.

ican society (and the whole Western World) would eventually collapse, but a long period of power and prosperity would intervene before the inevitable catastrophe if America succeeded in dominating Asia.[7] For Henry, imperialism was simply another indication not of an historical cycle but of that approaching world death which no human actions could forestall. Like Twain, however, and unlike his brother, Henry Adams was unable to find a psychological and philosophical refuge in his mechanistic system. In a significant letter dated November 18, 1901, Brooks himself pointed out to his brother the differences in their positions:

> In theory you believe as I do that men are automatic, that we cannot do otherwise than we do—that there is no advance and in practice you are always worrying for an American Eutopia. You complain because we don't find something new under the sun. Dear man—we are only repeating Babylon. We are going over the same ground only faster. Were you to discover Eutopia, nature would stop. There can be no American system. It's a contradiction to every philosophical principle. We are having our little day just now. Let us thank God and enjoy it. Those who follow will pay. We may shine through.[8]

For Henry Adams as for Mark Twain, a personal sense of guilt and the overriding power of the American Dream (the two blend imperceptibly in a curious fashion) were stronger than the amorality to which their deterministic positions lent themselves. Although both men had moments of appearing to revel in their front row seats to the imminent götterdämmerung, both were agonized by their awareness of the human cost of such a performance. Theo-

7. See Arthur F. Beringause, *Brooks Adams* (New York, Knopf, 1955), p. 143 and passim.

8. Adams Collection, quoted in Beringause, p. 233.

retically it should have been comforting that the historical process was merely an extension of biology or physics; one suspects the need for this kind of consolation behind Adams' and Twain's frantic search for "laws." Actually, for minds steeped in the Enlightenment, history could never be less than moral—even when it came to teach the most appalling lessons.

Before our own *fin de siècle* imperialism disillusioned Twain with the American historical experiment, the actions of the European powers had already made him more aware of the ironies and complexities involved in the entire process of history; and this awareness, in turn, became an important factor in his growing philosophical pessimism. Typical of the period of the late nineties is a little sketch called "The Dervish and the Offensive Stranger." Every act, says Twain's spokesman in the sketch, has both good and evil results, and these results "breed on and on, century after century." But what are good and evil acts and good and evil results? It is "good," Twain argues, that 400,000,000 Chinese have escaped our civilization; it is "bad" that 100,000 Chinese have become Christians (*29*, 311–14). In his letters of the period and in *Following the Equator* he wrestled with similar tortuous paradoxes as he was forced to take sides in what seemed to him a contest between real barbarism and cruel, hypocritical, and greedy civilization. But what is most significant about these early discussions of imperialism is that Twain, for the first time in his writing, began overtly to suggest the futility and repetitiveness of history. America's seizure of the Philippines, in a sense, merely clarified the whole issue; he was now free to abandon the last shreds of his belief in linearity.

In the most general terms, it might be said that imperialism forced Twain to reconcile and coalesce his theory of history with a conception of human nature that all his life had tended to be dark. The Whig progressivist, we must recall, attempted to link moral with intellectual and material progress by assuming that the growth of knowledge would produce better men through the development of better institutions; the latter, indeed (to use Twain's classic phrase) would be nothing more than "man-factories." However preoccupied he was with such ideas in the 1880's and 1890's, Twain, at the same time, was becoming more and more convinced of the general baseness of mankind at all times and places. During a journey down the Rhone in September of 1891, for example, he wrote his wife that he had seen a hill full of ruins dating from Roman times, a hill which had been a scene of slaughter and burning from the time of the Romans to that of the Crusaders. "These are pathetic shores," he remarked, "and they make one despise the human race" (*35*, 553). While reminiscent of his familiar attacks on the Middle Ages, such a comment is, of course, far more sweeping and inclusive. It points in an entirely different direction from notes such as his reference to "the age of pious w - - - - s" in the margin of his *Saint-Simon*.

For Twain as for Joseph Conrad, the barbarism of many of the imperialist adventures simply stripped the last veneer of civilization from nineteenth-century man and exposed the unchanging savagery underneath. In *Heart of Darkness* Conrad has Kurtz, the "emissary of pity, and science, and progress," look into his own soul as he lies dying and see "the horror!" [9] Observing the white man at work, not only in the Belgian Congo but in the Philippines and China, Twain also was quick to see the horror. Historical parallels sprang into the minds of both writers. Conrad recalls how the "decent young citizen in a toga" had quickly reverted to savagery when offered the temptation, and in his later writing Twain likewise stressed the continuity of human nature. Angered by religious persecution on Crete in 1905, he wrote that the fanatic was slaughtering unbelievers "in

9. New York, New American Library (1950), pp. 82, 133.

the time of the Caesars . . . in Mahomet's time . . . in the time of the Inquisition . . . in France a couple of centuries . . . in England in Mary's day, he has been at it ever since he saw the light, he is at it today in Crete . . . he will be at it somewhere else tomorrow." Nor was fanaticism the only human constant. When man was not calculatingly or wantonly cruel, he was money-mad: "There is not an acre of ground on the globe that is in possession of its rightful owner, or has not been taken away from owner after owner, cycle after cycle, by force and bloodshed." [1]

To believe in the moral progress of man in the face of such timeless depravity was inconceivable. In a reply to an item quoted in a Presbyterian newspaper to the effect that man is "the chief love and delight of God" Twain wrote:

> when I am feeling historical, there is nothing that ecstatifies me like hunting the Chief Love and Delight of God around and around . . . I watch him progressing and progressing—always progressing—always mounting higher and higher, sometimes by means of the Terror, sometimes by eight hundred years of witch-burning, sometimes by help of a St. Bartholomew's, sometimes by spreading hell and civilization in China, sometimes by preserving and elevating the same at home by a million soldiers and a thousand battleships; and when we get around to today I still look at him spread out over the whole page of the morning paper, grabbing in Congress . . . lynching the innocent, slobbering hypocrisies, reeking, dripping, unsavory, but always recognizable as . . . the Chief Love and Delight of God.[2]

1. "The Lowest Animal," in "Letters from the Earth," pp. 286–95. According to De Voto the sketch may date from earlier troubles on Crete in 1897.

2. *Mark Twain in Eruption*, ed. Bernard De Voto (New York, Harper, 1940), pp. 383–4.

In this passage, imperialism has become part of the general nightmare of history, which in turn has merged imperceptibly into a more comprehensive philosophy of life. Not only is man really (to use Twain's phrase) "the lowest Animal" in the universe, but he is doomed to remain at the bottom of the evolutionary scale; he cannot hope to raise himself.

Boldly Twain slashed at the Gordian knot linking the growth of knowledge with moral progress. "It is not worth while to try to keep history from repeating itself," he wrote in 1907,

> for man's character will always make the preventing of the repetitions impossible. Whenever man makes a large stride in material prosperity and progress he is sure to think that *he* has progressed whereas he has not advanced an inch; nothing has progressed but his circumstances. *He* stands where he stood before. He knows more than his forebears knew but his intellect is no better than theirs and never will be. He is richer than his forebears but his character is no improvement upon theirs. Riches and education are not a permanent possession; they will pass away, as in the case of Rome and Greece and Egypt and Babylon; and a moral and mental midnight will follow—with a dull long sleep and a slow reawakening. From time to time he makes what looks like a real change in his character but it is not a real change; and it is only transitory anyway . . . circumstances are stronger than he and all his works.[3]

That this passage is a blunt repudiation of the dream of the Enlightenment is clear enough. What is considerably less clear is the precise nature of the theory of history that is being substituted. The language, the repetition of words and phrases, the very rhythm of many of the lines betray

3. Ibid., p. 66.

Twain's own uncertainty, an uncertainty he was never completely successful in resolving. All we can note with any assurance is that this passage seems to point in two directions, both of them relevant to much of Twain's later thought. On the one hand, there is more than a hint of that theory of history which we have already observed Twain elaborating elsewhere: civilizations rise and fall, human character *seems* to progress or progresses for a short while (at least to the extent that "civilization" can be differentiated from "mental and moral midnight") until there arise those circumstances (e.g. material prosperity and such signs of social complexity as the development of classes and centralization) which prey on basic human weaknesses (e.g. greed and love of power—or the reverence of power) and draw men back into barbarism. On such a theory of history Twain could logically postulate the early glory of science and—as he often did to the very end of his life—an idyllic Jeffersonian America, a simple and slumbering Eden, which could be superimposed on childhood memories of Hannibal.

On the other hand, perhaps human character simply did not ameliorate, perhaps (as the Professor of the Science of Historical Forecast declares) "the average man remains exactly the same" and "even extraordinary people are eternally repeated in the same proportions." [4] If this were true, civilization at any time and place was nothing but the hypocritical mask worn by man to conceal the baseness of his thoughts and the meanness and cruelty of his actions. The function of the honest writer was to tear away the mask. Twain was impelled late in life to violate the idyllic image of Hannibal repeatedly, even compulsively, in such works as *Pudd'nhead Wilson, The Mysterious Stranger,* and "The Man that Corrupted Hadleyburg." He even came to the defense of Zola's *La Terre,* because, he noted, there was nothing in the book that had not happened in the average

4. "Letters from the Earth," pp. 138–40.

American village. Zola "exposed your own people to you." [5] Hannibal, in short, was not the most idyllic of societies, only the most hypocritical; essentially it was every town, anywhere, anytime. As a complex of meaningful and distinctive historical values, however, it had ceased to exist. "Nature has no originality," says Twain's Professor. "Everything happens again and yet again—monotonously." [6] Or, as Twain scrawled bitterly and sardonically in the margin of a book by an optimistic evolutionist: "The world was made for man, and man was made to suffer and be damned." [7] The final meaning of history was that history, at least in human terms, had no meaning.

In the face of such a vision of the emptiness of temporal existence, human beings from Plato and the Eastern mystics to Nietzsche and Eliot have sought in their various fashions to escape from the wheel of time into a realm of more substantial values. For the later Twain, escape was an obsessive need; yet we shall have occasion to note that it existed as a powerful impulse even when his faith in history appeared most firm. Indeed, any simple chronological division of Twain's thought permits us to point tendencies, to isolate theories and note influences only at the expense of ignoring the complexity, at any given time, of his response to human experience and the artistic problems (often unsolved) posed to his work by this complexity. We must now turn our attention, therefore, to certain of Twain's major texts, in the hope of observing his images of history as they operate within a concrete literary framework.

5. Ibid., pp. 279–92. For a detailed analysis of Twain's changing image of Hannibal see Henry N. Smith, "Mark Twain's Images of Hannibal: From St. Petersburg to Eseldorf," Gayley Lecture, Univ. of California, 1956, subsequently published in *Texas Studies in English*, 37 (1958), 3–23.

6. "Letters from the Earth," pp. 138–40.

7. Alexander Winchell, *Sketches of Creation* (New York, 1909), p. 332; MTP.

Part Two

THE HIGH COST OF PROGRESS

4.

THE AMERICAN AS DREAMER: EARLY TRAVEL BOOKS AND *The Gilded Age*

As a young writer Twain aggressively shared the intellectual assumption of his age that history was the mere record of the development of institutions toward perfection. Because of this assumption, the past, in Twain's earliest work, retained no positive value except a fugitive aesthetic appeal; it was often amusing, sometimes horrible—seldom really important. Humor and disgust are the dominant notes of *The Innocents Abroad.* The force of his almost unexamined convictions about history adds a certain strength to the book which is missing from, let us say, *A Connecticut Yankee,* where these convictions are more overt but less instinctively believed in. In *The Innocents Abroad* chivalry is ridiculed, gladiatorial combats are brilliantly burlesqued, and Europeans and Middle Easterners are attacked on various occasions for their poverty, backwardness, filth, lack of industry, and ignorance. Only here and there in Europe was the light of modern civilization beginning to dawn in the persons of such figures as Louis Napoleon and a certain Russian nobleman whom Twain described approvingly as a "man of progress and enterprise—a representative man of the age. He is the Chief Director of the railway system of

Russia—a sort of railroad king. In his line he is making things move along in this country. He has travelled extensively in America" (2, 118).

Like the Yankee whom they so much resemble, both these men were far more representative of technology than of political democracy; for the latter Twain had deep reservations during this period in his life.[1] For technology, however, he had an enthusiasm born of both personal fascination and conviction. In a letter (1867) to the *Alta Californian*, for example, he relates how he spent the night at a General Singleton's near Quincy, Illinois. Singleton, "one of the farmer-princes of Illinois," apparently lit his house with gas made on the premises from the refuse of petroleum; and, after an elaborate description of the gas-making apparatus, Twain is impelled to comment: "I don't take any interest in prize bulls, astonishing jackasses and prodigious crops, but I took a strong fancy to that gas apparatus." Quincy itself he called "a wonderful place. It has always thrived—sometimes slowly and steadily, sometimes with a rush—but always making an unquestionable progress . . . It is the second city of Illinois, in population, business, activity and enterprise, and high promise for the future." These remarks on Quincy, it should be noted, come immediately after a noncommittal description of how the railroad (that "ravenous destroyer of towns") had wiped

1. For further comparison between Louis Napoleon and the Yankee see below, p. 119. In *Letters from the Sandwich Islands* (San Francisco, Grabhorn Press, 1937), pp. 81–2, Twain's comment on the policies of King Kamehameha IV of Hawaii suggests his attitude toward democracy in 1866: "He took back a good deal of power which his predecessors had surrendered to the people, abolished the universal suffrage clause and denied the privilege of voting to all save such as were possessed of a hundred dollars' worth of real estate or had an income of seventy-five dollars a year. And, if my opinion were asked, I would say he did a wise thing in this last named matter." His son (the ruler in 1866) Twain goes on to note, "is invested with very great power. But he is a man of good sense and excellent education, and has an extended knowledge of business . . . and therefore he uses his vast authority wisely and well."

out Hannibal's prosperity after a period of temporary growth. At this time in his life, in other words, the past lacked even a nostalgic attraction for Twain. Pale too were God and the wonders of God beside the new technology, "This modern navigation out-wonders any wonder the scriptural writers dreampt [sic] of," he wrote in another letter to the *Alta* while still on the ship carrying him away from San Francisco. "Verily, with his imperial intellect and his deep-searching wisdom, man is almost a God!" [2]

In view of such sentiments, it is not surprising that the early Twain was thoroughly anti-primitivistic. He savagely ridiculed Cooper's Indians: they are dead, he noted, "died with their creator." [3] Likewise, although he personally found missionaries bigoted and puritanical, he defended their work in the Hawaiian Islands as a civilizing influence. The progress of the natives from slavery to civilization, Twain wrote, "must shame the cheap inventions of romancers." [4] Elsewhere, after describing the ancient funeral orgies of the natives, he commented pointedly: "They were not the salt of the earth, those 'gentle children of the sun' " (*4*, 224).

Occasionally, however, Twain's ambivalence toward missionaries leads him (at least potentially) into a more complex view of history. "Nearby is an interesting ruin," he wrote in one letter to the *Sacramento Weekly Union* (1866),

> . . . a place where human sacrifices were offered up in those old bygone days when the simple child of nature, yielding momentarily to sin when sorely

2. *Mark Twain's Travels with Mr. Brown,* ed. Franklin Walker and G. Ezra Dane (New York, Knopf, 1940), pp. 77–8, 145–8.

3. Ibid., p. 266. With regard to Indians, Twain's western trip naturally proved a particularly disenchanting experience (see *3*, 131–5).

4. *Letters,* pp. 82–3. For his comments on missionaries see pp. 98–104, 116–18.

> tempted, acknowledged his error when calm reflection had shown it to him, and came forward with noble frankness and offered up his grandmother as an atoning sacrifice—in those old days when the luckless sinner could keep on cleansing his conscience and achieving periodical happiness as long as his relations held out; long before the missionaries braved a thousand privations to come and make them permanently miserable by telling them how beautiful and blissful a place heaven is, and how nearly impossible it is to get there; and showed the poor native how dreary a place perdition is and what unnecessarily liberal facilities there are for going to it; showed him how, in his ignorance, he had gone and fooled away all his kin-folks to no purpose; showed him what rapture it is to work all day long for fifty cents to buy food for the next day with, as compared with fishing for pastime and lolling in the shade through eternal Summer, and eating of the bounty that nobody labored to provide but Nature.

In this passage—where the focus is not on laws and education, but religious belief and human nature—Twain's irony cuts down both Noble Savage and Puritan, even the latter's industriousness which he so warmly praises elsewhere.

On the following page, however, the focus quickly shifts back to the legal and intellectual progress of modern civilization and the irony is accordingly quickly dissipated in a burst of approval. Twain describes the savagery and rigor of life in the ancient Hawaiian kingdom and then comments characteristically:

> The missionaries have clothed them [i.e. the common people], educated them, broken up the tyrannous authority of their chiefs, and given them freedom and

> the right to enjoy whatever the labor of their hand and brain produces, with equal laws for all and punishment for all alike who transgress them. . . . The wonderful benefit conferred upon these people by the missionaries is so prominent, so palpable and so unquestionable, that the frankest compliment I can pay them . . . is simply to point to the condition of the Sandwich Islanders of Captain Cook's time, and their condition today. Their work speaks for itself.[5]

Actually, of course, the work of the missionaries told Twain only what he wanted to hear. Throughout his life he was continually debating the value of their work, and his conclusions on any given occasion naturally reflected very closely his changing conceptions of history.

Significantly, even in his earliest writings Twain had no strong convictions regarding the perfectibility of human nature—that important corollary to the idea of the progress of civilization. He was sure that (as he puts it in *The Innocents Abroad*) "in America the people are absolutely wiser and know much more than their grandfathers did" (*1*, 280). He was perfectly willing to speculate that the oppressed peasantry of the Ottoman empire, "with education and liberty, would be a happy and contented race" (*2*, 165). Yet he sensed at the same time the profound quality of inertia in human nature. In *Roughing It,* for example, in the course of a description of the joys of camping out, Twain observed that "we are descended from desert-lounging Arabs, and countless ages of growth toward perfect civilization have failed to root out of us the nomadic instinct" (*3*, 192). This same idea he had first broached from a rather different point of view in *The Innocents Abroad.* Alluding to the side-trips the "pilgrims" had taken on horseback throughout Palestine, he remarked that "it was

5. Ibid., pp. 40–2. For later, significant changes in his attitude toward the civilizing of native races see below, pp. 192–4.

painful to note how readily these town bred men had taken to the free life of the camp and desert. The nomadic instinct is a human instinct; it was born with Adam and transmitted through the patriarchs, and after thirty centuries of steady effort, civilization has not educated it entirely out of us yet . . . The nomadic instinct cannot be educated out of an Indian at all" (2, 333–4). The images of nomadism and freedom from social convention in this passage are, of course, those which in Twain's later work become such an important counterpoise to his commitment to the historical process. Here, however, they merely serve to deny the efficacy of history, without themselves taking on a positive value; Twain was chiefly concerned with recording his contempt for the pious gentility of the pilgrims. In *Roughing It* the difference in tone with which the same materials are treated is perhaps indicative of a significant change in emphasis: freedom, in the later book, is a rich and exhilarating component of a realm of experience closed to the "town-bred" man.[6]

Another comment in *The Innocents Abroad* is more explicit and concedes a good deal less to the educative influence of civilization. "With all respect for those ancient Israelites," Twain writes in the course of retelling the story of Jeroboam and the golden calf, "I cannot overlook the fact that they were not always virtuous enough to withstand the seductions of a golden calf. Human nature has not changed much since then" (2, 207). Even in his first work, Twain's conception of human nature was thus at

6. See Henry N. Smith, "Mark Twain as an Interpreter of the Far West: The Structure of *Roughing It*," in *The Frontier in Perspective*, ed. Walker D. Wyman and Clifton B. Kroeber (Madison, 1957), pp. 212–18. As a description of the lives of Arabs and plains Indians, the concept of nomadic primitivism was a conventional enough one for the eighteenth- and nineteenth-century writer—which suggests that there are roots to Twain's mature primitivism which touch sources other than simply childhood memories or even the mythology of the Mississippi River.

least potentially in conflict with his conception of history. Very early, in other words, he tended to divorce the Enlightenment idea of progress from one of its key assumptions; instead he gave added weight to education, legal and political development, and, above all, technology. This was, of course, no real solution to a problem that was to play an increasingly central role in his mind and art.

The major conflict in *The Innocents Abroad,* however—a conflict which had important repercussions on the style of the book—is not between two conceptions of human experience but between Twain's moral convictions and his empirical point of view on the one hand and his aesthetic instincts on the other. The past might be humorous or terrible, it could often be dismissed with a joke or a grimace, but there was no denying that it possessed an aesthetic dimension almost totally absent from the world of 1860. Twain's dilemma is a reflection of the same cultural problem which we have already noted in Cooper and Irving.[7] The American Adam was a practical man, an inventor and a doer; he had rejected the past because the past was evil and corrupt, and as a democrat he rejoiced that his country lacked the moldering artifacts symbolic of tyranny and despotism but so necessary to the picturesque canon. Admittedly deficient for these reasons in aesthetic sensibility (or lacking objects for contemplation should he, by chance, possess such a sensibility), the American could only point to his moral superiority and his efforts on behalf of modern civilization. This was Twain's plea for himself and the Yankee: it was James' for Christopher Newman. When confronted with art tainted by the moral corruption of the society it reflects, the independent and pure-minded American would do well to keep it at arm's length. In *The Innocents Abroad* Twain acknowledges that some of the paintings of the old masters in the Louvre are beautiful, but he

7. See above, pp. 16–18.

is quick to add: "at the same time they carried such evidences about them of the cringing spirit of those great men that we found small pleasure in examining them. Their nauseous adulation of princely patrons was more prominent to me and chained my attention more surely than the charms of color and expression which are claimed to be in the picture" (*1*, 131). Similarly, Versailles is beautiful, but he cannot really forget (though he wants to) that it was built with the suffering of thousands (*1*, 150–1).

The subject matter of the old masters was consistently distressing. There were too many aristocrats (*1*, 267–8), too many Virgins, popes, and "saintly scare-crows" painted, while stirring scenes from classical civilization were almost ignored (*2*, 7–8). Here as always in Twain's work the past really being attacked was the Catholic Middle Ages and Renaissance. Italy had been groping "in the midnight of priestly superstition for sixteen hundred years" (*1*, 263); it was "one vast museum of magnificence and misery . . . the wretchedest, princeliest land on earth," full of sloth and ignorance (*1*, 266). For Roman art and civilization, however, Twain had far more favorable comment. He praised the industry of the ancient Pompeiians; the very ruts preserved in the streets testified that "they were not lazy. They hurried in those days. . . . They would not go around when it was quicker to go through. We do that way in our cities." The frescoes at Pompeii "are often much more pleasing than the celebrated rubbish of the old masters of three centuries ago" (*2*, 36–8). Classical art had a vital message for the practical American, but endless "imaginary portraits" of martyrs at best offered him "nothing tangible," nothing he could "grasp and take a living interest in" (*1*, 242).

Everywhere in *The Innocents Abroad* Twain begged his fellow Americans to measure Europe and the Middle East with the empirical yardstick. The preface makes explicit the purpose of the book: "to suggest to the reader how *he* would be likely to see Europe and the East if he looked at them with his own eyes instead of the eyes of those who travelled in those countries before him" (*1*, xxi). Savagely, he attacked the cant of art criticism and in particular the hypocrisy of those Americans who expressed for European masterpieces a delight which they did not really feel or which the facts of the situation could not sustain. This hypocrisy was a betrayal of the present and future for two reasons: on the one hand, it implied a reverence for the past that stultified creativity; on the other, it assumed values for the past which, in many cases, could not be empirically proven.[8] At the same time, Twain was well aware of his own cultural limitations and, by extension, those of most Americans. "One has no opportunity in America to acquire a critical judgement in art," he noted at one point in *The Innocents Abroad* (*1*, 242); and he candidly admitted after praising Italian railways: "These things win me more than Italy's hundred galleries of priceless art treasures, because I can understand the one and am not competent to appreciate the other" (*1*, 262). In Rome Twain said that he "felt all the time like a boy in a candy-shop—there was everything to choose from and yet no choice" (*2*, 12). James' Christopher Newman, we must recall, also felt like a "little child" in Paris.[9]

The aesthetic deficiency Twain sensed in himself he explained as characteristic of America and Americans because of the bent of the American mind. He praised the papal government for its art collection:

8. Of Da Vinci's "The Last Supper": "The world seems to have become settled in the belief, long ago, that it is not possible for human genius to outdo this creation of Da Vinci's." My comments draw heavily on Twain's extended discussion of "The Last Supper" (*1*, 188–95).

9. *The American* (Boston and New York, 1907), p. 28.

> The popes have long been the patrons and preservers of art, just as our new, practical Republic is the encourager and upholder of mechanics. In their Vatican is stored up all that is curious and beautiful in art; in our Patent Office is hoarded all that is curious or useful in mechanics . . . We can make something of a guess at a man's character by the style of nose he carries on his face. The Vatican and the Patent Office are governmental noses, and they bear a deal of character about them. [2, 8]

The lines are clearly drawn in this passage between the old and the beautiful and the new and the useful—between an aesthetically and technologically oriented world. Tangible attempts at reconciliation could only lead to anachronism. Of the National Academy of Design, built in the "Moorish" style, Twain wrote: "as if the atmosphere of antiquity and poetry and romance, that cast a charm around that style in its ancient home beyond the seas, could be reproduced here in the midst of railroads and steamboats, and business rush and clamor, and acres of brownstone fronts—as if it could be anything but clownish and repulsive without that atmosphere." [1] To the modern reader this sounds like the familiar plea for an indigenous art, but actually it is far closer to an admission that the creation of any kind of beauty was impossible to the civilization America was bringing into being.

Implicit in Twain's thinking is the sharp dichotomy—heightened but not initiated by the Romantic movement—between reason and imagination, objective and subjective experience and the dangerous tendency to dissociate the two while making art the product of the higher or (depending on one's point of view) lower imaginative world. Equally implicit is a central though usually unacknowl-

1. *Travels with Mr. Brown,* p. 242.

edged assumption of the picturesque canon: that beauty consists in "an intellectual rather than visual predilection for certain subjects." [2] Americans could not be both empirical and artistic; through circumstance and moral conviction they were completely conditioned by the "real" present, whereas imaginative faculties only flourished in constant contact with the "unreal," intangible yet richly associative past. At the same time, actual relics of the past could only generate beauty when freed of their material dross by the transmutive power of the imagination. "Everywhere was dirt and dust and dinginess and gloom," Twain wrote of the inside of St. Sophia; "everywhere were signs of a hoary antiquity, but with nothing touching or beautiful about it" (2, 72). Damascus, on the other hand, he first saw from high in the mountains as a "great white city" surrounded by a "billowy expanse of green foliage." Distance, he noted, softened the picture and cast "over it and above it a drowsing air of repose to spiritualize it and make it seem rather a beautiful estray from the mysterious worlds we visit in dreams than a substantial tenant of our coarse, dull globe" (2, 177).

The American, in short, could satisfy whatever aesthetic propensities he had only during rare, fortuitous moments of imaginative escape from the mundane world. Twain, for example, found the Sea of Galilee neither striking nor beautiful "to one's actual vision" and attacked previous writers who had described it in glowing terms. Yet he goes on to observe that

> night is the time to see Galilee. Gennesaret under these lustrous stars has nothing repulsive about it. Gennesaret with the glittering reflections of the constellations flecking its surface, almost makes me regret I ever saw the rude glare of the day upon it. Its history

2. Mario Praz, *The Romantic Agony* (New York, Meridian, 1956), p. 20, n. 15.

> and its associations are its chiefest charm, in any eyes, and the spells they weave are feeble in the searching light of the sun. *Then,* we scarcely feel the fetters. Our thoughts wander constantly to the practical concerns of life, and refuse to dwell upon things that seem vague and unreal. But when the day is done, even the most unimpressionable must yield to the dreamy influences of this tranquil starlight. The old traditions of the place steal upon his memory and haunt his reveries, and then his fancy clothes all sights and sounds with the supernatural. [2, 243–5]

Here it is the associative function of the imagination that is freed by the immaterializing power of night. The aesthetic moment is one of escape from the tyranny of time and reality.[3] Twain's continual use of the image of sleep and dreaming to describe these moments is particularly significant in the light of the importance assumed by this image in his later work. As he employs it, the image always has connotations of some kind of unreality and stasis: qualities of life that are far removed from the empirical, dynamic world of modern industrial civilization. Applied to experience in general, it suggests, in Twain's writing, the aesthetic dimension. Applied to a society, it suggests a state of arrested historical development or (to put it another way) a state of remoteness and isolation from the main stream of

3. The best example of this quality of temporal suspension is found in Twain's sketch "A Memorable Midnight Experience" (1872). He tells of an evening visit to Westminster Abbey and the tombs of the poets and kings. While looking at the statuary figure of Queen Eleanor of Aquitaine he and his companions see the clock face of Parliament House glowing through the window of the Abbey and pointing to midnight: "It was a decisive reminder that we were a part of this present sordid, plodding, commonplace time, and not august relics of a bygone age and the comrades of kings—and then the booming of the great bell tolled twelve, and with the last stroke, the mocking clock face vanished in sudden darkness and left us with the past and its grandeurs again" (*29,* 10).

history—Hannibal before the Civil War, Arthur's Britain, Pitcairn's Island. Applied, finally, to the life of individuals, it suggests not a social, but a metaphysical stasis—a mode of eternity.[4]

Terence Martin has demonstrated that the imagery of sleep, indolence, night, and shadows used to symbolize a realm of imaginative experience foreign to the bustling, "daylight" American world is common to the work of earlier writers such as Brown, Poe, Irving, and Hawthorne.[5] Certainly it is everywhere in *The Innocents Abroad:* Versailles was "an exquisite dream" (*1,* 149); Milan Cathedral, a "fairy delusion" (*1,* 170); Palestine, "no more of this work-day world . . . it is dreamland" (*2,* 359); the banks of the Rhone offered "visions of fabled fairy-land" (*1,* 98). Necessarily, however, such visions could only be fleeting and attenuated. Twain relates how at Pompeii he went "dreaming among the trees" until a train whistle woke him up and reminded him that he "belonged in the nineteenth century, and was not a dusty mummy." And he adds: "The idea of a railroad train actually running to old dead Pompeii, and whistling irreverently and calling for passengers in the most bustling and business-like way, was as unpoetical and disagreeable as it was strange" (*2,* 42). Obviously the gap between the two modes of experience was absolute and unbridgeable. From the material of history the imagination, in moments of reverie, could create a picturesque and romantic dream world, but from present reality the picturesque and romantic were totally absent.

Each mode of experience, moreover, seemed to demand a separate style of prose. To be sure, this is by no means the sole cause of the wide stylistic fluctuation in *The Innocents*

4. Twain also associates this image with childhood, described in *The Innocents Abroad* (*2,* 129) and elsewhere as a time of dreaming.

5. "Rip, Ichabod, and the American Imagination," *American Literature, 31* (1959), 137–49.

Abroad. Twain was young, unsure of his status and place as a writer, and freely experimenting with the various literary conventions with which he was familiar—from the picturesque to western humor.[6] Nevertheless, he fairly consistently mingles utilitarian and often humorous and debunking descriptions of what he actually saw in the world around him with purple passages appropriate to the reveries occasioned by historical associations. Thus he can write of the Italian town of Civita Vecchia:

> There is nothing here to see. They have not even a cathedral, with eleven tons of solid silver archbishops in the back room; and they do not show you any moldy buildings that are seven thousand years old; nor any smoke-dried old fire-screens which are *chef d'oeuvres* of Rubens or Simpson, or Titian or Ferguson, or any of those parties; and they haven't any bottled fragments of saints, and not even a nail from the true cross. [*1*, 273]

Twain in this passage is the practical, hard-headed American observer of things as they are. Yet a few pages earlier the sight of an Etruscan tear-jug had called forth the following:

> It spoke to us in a language of its own; and with a pathos more tender than any words might bring, its mute eloquence swept down the long roll of the centuries with its tale of a vacant chair, a familiar footstep missed from the threshold, a pleasant voice gone from the chorus, a vanished form! . . . No shrewdly-worded history could have brought the myths and shadows of that old dreamy age before us clothed with human flesh and warmed with human sympathies so

6. I am indebted to Henry Nash Smith for having first pointed out to me the problem of style in *The Innocents Abroad* and Twain's particular conception of aesthetic experience.

> vividly as did this poor little unsentient vessel of pottery. [*1*, 259]

Here Twain is attempting to describe not what he sees but the shadowy, vaguely romantic, and pathetic (and wholly imaginary) set of associations that according to the picturesque canon make the vase a thing of beauty. The result is a shockingly different style of writing.

Twain himself must have sensed that a dual style was no real solution to the dilemma of a writer who could find no aesthetic dimension in the moral, political, and social position he was committed to defend. In passage after passage he undercut his own solemnity; as a practical American he was half-conscious of its absurdity and its obsolescence.[7] Only later in *Huckleberry Finn* was he able to shape the vernacular into a vehicle for conveying the beauty as well as the ugliness and terror of a real world, but even in this book his spokesman is a young boy describing the America of 1835. Advancing years and, in particular, his return to the Mississippi in 1882 only increased his conviction that the utilitarian present had destroyed important qualities of beauty in the past.[8] By the time he wrote *Huckleberry Finn,* moreover, his dream of beauty had become part of a more comprehensive idyll.

As early as the 1870's Twain's image of the dream had begun to take on a social as well as an aesthetic meaning, because of his growing awareness of the positive values to be found in his own personal past and that of America in general (even, indeed, that of England). Reasons for this new sensitivity are not hard to discover. In the first place, having married into stable, quiet upper-middle class respectability, he began to be afflicted with nostalgia for the adventures of his youth. *Roughing It,* as James Cox has

7. See, e.g., *1*, 10; *2*, 26.

8. See Leo Marx, "The Pilot and the Passenger: Landscape Conventions and the Style of *Huckleberry Finn,*" *American Literature,* 27 (1956), 136–43.

noted, is already redolent with such nostalgia for the remote experiences of a vanished era.[9] At the same time, his cordial reception by the English during extended visits in 1872 and 1873 was having a significant influence on his political opinions and his conception of the Old World. Westminster Abbey, for example, after a dramatic midnight visit seemed to him "no longer a grisly museum of moldering vanities, but her better and worthier self—the deathless mentor of a great nation, the guide and encourager of right ambitions, the preserver of just fame, and the home and refuge for the nation's best and bravest when their work is done" (*29,* 13). His pro-English sentiments were translated into an advocacy of reverence for "the old and great" and into a distaste for popular democracy (in this case making firmer beliefs he already held) and for "this present sordid, plodding, commonplace time." [1]

Finally, of course, like so many other honest and sensitive men of his generation, Twain was increasingly disgusted with the corruption of post-Civil War America, and this too impelled him to discover the values of the past. Progress was not disavowed but it could not longer be blandly assumed.[2] In a speech prepared for delivery to a gathering of Americans in London on July 4, 1872, Twain noted ironically that "this is an age of progress and ours is a progressive land." He then proceeded to list the various abuses of the time (and prominent American heroes of different eras

9. "Mark Twain: A Study in Nostalgia" (diss., Indiana, 1955), p. 40.

1. Twain's pro-English sentiments are extensively documented in Howard Baetzhold, "Mark Twain: England's Advocate," *American Literature, 28* (1956), 328–46.

2. As Cox puts it (p. 30): "from the time of the California gold rush to the end of the century there co-exists with the American dream of Paradise and Youth the Nightmare of the Fall and Old Age. The dream of the future becomes the dream of the past; the spirit of hope is transformed into nostalgic memory." The best study of Twain's political ideas of the 1870's and their cultural context is Kenneth B. Andrews, *Nook Farm: Mark Twain's Literary Circle,* Cambridge, Mass., 1950.

such as Washington, Franklin, Tweed, Gould, Pomeroy) and concluded by remarking that "we may find hope for the future in the fact that as unhappy as is the condition of our political morality today, England has risen out of a far fouler since the days when Charles I enobled courtesans and all political places was a matter of bargain and sale. There is hope for us yet" (*28*, 35–6). Actually, in this speech he was directing his main appeal not so much to the future as to the past or at least (to state the matter perhaps more accurately) to a future that would have regained certain cherished qualities of the past. As he wrote elsewhere in the course of a description of British veneration for Wellington: "while Wellington is justly still in fashion here in England, Washington is fading out of the fashion with us. It is not a good sign. The idols we have raised in his stead are not to our honor" (*29*, 63).

What Twain and others were lamenting was the passing of the allegedly simpler, stabler, "dreaming" American society of before the Civil War. His sleep-dream metaphor was an effort to render concrete the quality of stasis implicit in the eighteenth-century theory of progress, especially as this theory was applied to America. Utopia was the America of 1825. The Jeffersonian tradition, as we have already noted, cherished simplicity and the "middle way" of life; it feared change (which could only be for the worse), complexity, and, above all, greed and oligarchy, which it associated with urbanization and assumed was a sign of the imminent decline and fall of a civilization. The definitive statement of this viewpoint in the troubled, depression-ridden 1870's was Henry George's *Progress and Poverty*. George warned his countrymen that they could no longer assume progress, that economic inequality was leading to corruption and despotism, that "the type of modern growth is the great city," that, finally, "the civilized world is trembling on the verge of a great movement. Either it must be a leap upward, which will open the way to advances yet undreamed of, or it must be a plunge downward which will carry us back toward barbarism." Recent critics of George have pointed out that his solution to this social crisis was as distinctly Jeffersonian as his analysis.[3]

Certainly it was the Jeffersonian vision of life that Twain celebrated so insistently in the 70's and was to reject in the 80's (only to seize upon occasionally again late in life): the "summer world . . . bright and fresh, and brimming with life" of *Tom Sawyer* (*8,* 12);[4] the white-washed village basking in the sun of the first pages of *Life on the Mississippi* (*12,* 32); the island paradise of Pitcairn, whose inhabitants "lived in a deep Sabbath tranquillity, far from the world and its ambitions and vexations, and neither knowing or caring what was going on in the mighty empires that lie beyond their limitless ocean solitudes." Infrequently a ship touched there, Twain goes on to note in his description of life on the island, "moved them [the islanders] with aged news of bloody battles, devastating epidemics, fallen thrones, and ruined dynasties . . . and sailed away, leaving them to retire into their peaceful dreams . . . once more" (*19,* 344–5). We sense in this passage (and in the whole drift of the ensuing story, in which the island is invaded by all the corrupting impedimenta of a complex European civilization) the deep impulse toward isolationism and "neutrality" of the American mind. Fundamentally this isolationism has been our attempt to avoid entanglement in the process of history—to suspend history and, if possible, escape from it altogether.

3. New York, Random House, 1938, pp. 527–43. See above, pp. 41–2.

4. Twain also notes in this same passage that "Cardiff Hill, beyond the village and above it, was green with vegetation, and it lay just far enough away to seem a Delectable Land, dreamy, reposeful, and inviting." Smith points out that "the St. Petersburg of the novel must be recognized as a deliberate creation, not an effort to reproduce the actual town of Hannibal" ("Mark Twain's Image of Hannibal," pp. 6–12).

The reverse of the dream image with its connotations of serenity and peace is the image of tumult and noise almost always used by Twain to describe modern technological civilization. The steam engine at Pompeii and the volcano about to erupt in the *Connecticut Yankee* are alike in the picture they present of bursting, roaring, tearing—and potentially destructive—energy. In *The Gilded Age* when Philip Sterling walks down Broadway enveloped in "the roar and hum of its multitudinous traffic," Twain and Warner comment: "To the young American, here or elsewhere, the paths to fortune are innumerable and all open; there is invitation in the air and success in all his wide horizon. He is embarrassed which to choose . . . He has no traditions to bind him or guide him, and his impulse is to break away from the occupation his father has followed" (5, 112–13). The scene, in effect, sets the theme of the book: the threat posed to traditional values by the forces engulfing the post-Civil War generation. Throughout the novel the nature of these values is made clear by the two important cultural groups into which the characters fall. The refined, humanistic Montagues, Boltons, Sterlings—all representative of the upper middle classes of eighteenth-century New England and Pennsylvania—were obviously Warner's particular social ideal. Twain's naturally lay more in the western backwoods communities, whose inhabitants he described as "uncouth and not cultivated, and not particularly industrious; but they were honest and straightforward, and their virtuous ways commanded respect" (5, 49). Twain's too, of course, is the opening picture of lazy slumbering Obedstown, East Tennessee.

Everywhere in *The Gilded Age* those with at least vestigial roots in the past are contrasted with the rootless. Ruth Bolton has a Quaker background and perseveres in her ideal of work and service although her father is almost destroyed by the fever of speculation. Philip Sterling, who (as his name implies) had learned New England principles "at his mother's knees," earns his fortune with his bare hands and his genuine scientific knowledge. Alice Montague and her family preserved the strength and integrity of Puritanism but had "thrown off its narrowness," and "were now blossoming under the generous modern influences." They had reached the ideal "middle station" in life; "having only riches enough to be able to gratify reasonable desires, and yet make their gratifications always a novelty and a pleasure, the family occupied that just mean . . . which is rarely attained, and still more rarely enjoyed without discontent" (5, 210–11). Squire Montague himself emerges as a simple "lawyer-farmer," but like the elder Bolton he also gets involved in speculation and begins to "have his serene old age disturbed by anxieties and by the hopes of a great stroke of luck" (6, 196). Significantly, Twain and Warner stress the ruralness of the Montagues as one key to their relative integrity. Alice, for example, is described as "one of those patriotic women in the rural districts, who think men still are selected for Congress on account of qualifications for the office" (6, 193).

Because of their tenacious sense of values, these people fare reasonably well, unlike the other characters of no traditions. Among the latter it is the Westerners who prove particularly vulnerable to corruption. Dilworthy is venal; Washington Hawkins, weak and improvident; Colonel Sellers, flamboyant but futile; finally, Laura, of literally no background (she is an orphan), a Madame Bovary-like figure who shapes her mind on reading "largely made up of romances . . . which fed her imagination with the most exaggerated notions of life, and showed her men and women in a very false sort of heroism" (5, 181). She is also well read in "modern works of fiction, written by her own sex," which give her an exaggerated idea of women's powers (5, 192). For all the melodramatics in which she gets involved, Laura remains the clearest image in *The Gilded Age* of freedom and energy without direction, integrity, and responsibility. But the whole drift of the book—indeed, the whole drift of Twain's thought during the 70's—is best summed up in the mocking words of a newspaper correspondent who tells Colonel Sellers that "John Jay and Benjamin Franklin were well enough in their day, but the nation has made progress since then" (*6*, 44–5). Twain was appalled by the spectacle of American greed. Not until he was even more appalled in the later 70's by the spectacle of European immorality did his conception of history swing back to a more purely progressivist position. By then, however, his view of human nature was steadily darkening, and it was necessary to dream a different kind of dream.

5.
THE ROMANCE OF THE RIVER: *Life on the Mississippi*

Life on the Mississippi is a transitional work in every sense of the word. One section, written in 1878, looks backward to the idealization of a village society; a second, written in 1883, looks forward both to the celebration of nineteenth-century progress and to something very different—a set of values which have a relation to an historical time and place but which, as they are developed by Twain, take on a profoundly unhistorical meaning. In Twain's hands, they become, indeed, an antidote to the false promises of history.

It is clear enough that between the writing of the first and the second sections of *Life on the Mississippi* Twain's impulse to idealize the village society of his youth had disappeared, to be replaced by an equally strong impulse to celebrate the burgeoning industrial America he saw all around him. Not so clear are the reasons for this transformation. It has been pointed out that when Twain returned to the river in 1882, he was a famous man, a sophisticated and traveled individual, and that, inevitably, a more mature point of view put childhood memories in a new perspective.[1]

1. This shift, some of the factors which caused it, and its effect on Twain's image of Hannibal have been carefully traced in Smith, "Mark Twain's Images of Hannibal," pp. 6–25. Smith describes how, in the decade from 1875 to 1885, the white-washed democratic little community of *Tom Sawyer*

What must be stressed, however, is that the Mississippi trip of 1882 rather *confirmed* than created Twain's new attitude toward the past and present of America; it had actually been developing all through the late 70's as an indirect response to his changing opinions about England and Europe.

At the same time that his dislike for the meanness and corruption of post-Civil War American life was reaching its peak in 1877, the seeds of a new attitude were being sown. He had begun to write *The Prince and the Pauper* and was immersing himself not only in the English histories of Hume and Froude but also in various books dealing with the *ancien régime* and the French Revolution.[2] The real change, however, came during and because of Twain's European tour of 1878–79. Prior to this time his notebooks had been filled with comments on the corruption of America. After a series of these comments comes the note: "Write an Englishman's Tour in America." If carried out, this suggestion would apparently have given us a kind of inverse *Connecticut Yankee*. Near this note is another which reads: "Leathers Earl of Durham." Fifteen years later these ideas were combined in *The American Claimant*. Written when Twain's enthusiasm for later nineteenth-century America was again waning, it is, indeed, an answer to the *Yankee*.

But, beginning emphatically in February 1879 (the date of his arrival in Paris), one finds page after page of scathing attacks on the licentiousness, cruelty, and corruption of the French past and present.[3] The causes of this Francophobia

changed, in Twain's imagination, into a typical dirty, backward southern town.

2. Notebook 11 (1877), pp. 24–5, and *Mark Twain to Mrs. Fairbanks,* ed. Dixon Wecter (San Marino, the Huntington Library, 1949), pp. 207–9. This letter, as Howard Baetzhold has noted, contains, besides a list of books that Twain had recently read, some of his severest strictures against republican government.

3. See Notebooks 12–14. With his traveling and his reading of medieval

are undoubtedly numerous and complex. Paine's explanation (for what it is worth) is that the foggy, rainy, chilly weather of his Paris sojourn soured him on the French (*31,* 641–2). Actually his attitude seems compounded from his reading, his personal discomfort, national stereotypes (especially, alleged French sexual promiscuity)—and perhaps the fact that his own reception was not as warm here as in England. Inevitably Twain's attitude toward France, partially based as it was on generalizations from reading history and novels, began to rub off more and more on the English. As early as 1879, for example, he says he has been reading *Tom Jones* and that the only character whom he likes and who is not a barbarian is Squire Western. Then follows a characteristic generalization: "The English ought not to patronize the Zulus . . . what they were between the Roman Invasion and the time within the memory of a centenarian was but a small improvement upon the Shoshone Indians." [4]

In any case, America now appeared in a different perspective. "Looking back over history, one is comforted," he wrote after the remark that "France has usually been governed by prostitutes." "Bad as our gov't is, it is a mighty improvement on olden times." And again, more positively: "Take America by & large & it is the most civilized of all nations. Pure-minded women are the rule, in every rank of life of the *native-born.* The men are clean-minded, too, beyond the world's average." [5] Even in "The Great Revolution in Pitcairn" (1879), although the villain is an American, the civilization he introduces, with its nobility, its talk of "unification," and its inevitable Social Democrat, is distinctly European.

---

materials, Twain's anti-Catholicism also begins to appear again in his notes.

4. Notebook 14, p. 4, published in *Mark Twain's Notebook,* ed. A. B. Paine (New York, Harpers, 1935), p. 150.

5. Notebook 14, pp. 23, 29. Italics are Twain's.

Here as elsewhere Twain's theories of history were ultimately predicated on the century and geographical location of the particular species of human corruption that most disturbed him at any given time. It was always a question of where the stress was thrown. History lost all positive meaning for him only when it became impossible to assign evil any kind of temporal or physical locus—even one that was tentative and subject to change. Thus we must not ignore the fact that Twain asked Grant in 1880 to save this country "from dishonor & shame & from industrial disaster." [6] Nevertheless, because of his growing concern with the iniquities of Europe, American governmental practices and American personal morality were taking on for Twain, at least in comparative terms, a new attractiveness.

Around 1880 he also returned to the theme of American technological development which forms so conspicuous a part of *The Innocents Abroad.* "1 or 200 years from now we shall have a pop[.] of 150 or 200,000,000" he writes, in the midst of his comments on the French, "& then we shall lead the fashions & be the center of intelligence." In another place he remarks that Americans praise everything English but that the English nation despises America and Americans. But "we shall presently be indifferent to being looked down upon by a nation no bigger and no better than our own. We made the telegraph a practical thing." There follows the usual catalogue of inventions. Still another note of 1880—"Don Quixote is defended against Arabian Nights Supernaturals by Telephone Telegraph etc. & successfully"—suggests not only the theme and plot of *A Connecticut Yankee* but the incidents in a sketch called the "Legend of the Spectacular Ruin" published earlier that same year in *A Tramp Abroad.* In the "Legend," a take-off on medieval romance, Twain's knightly hero is a despised "man of science," who fights dragons by inductive methods

6. Notebook 15, p. 13.

—who "had brought brains to his aid." "He said he might be a little in advance of his age, but no matter—science would come to be honored, some time or other" (*9*, 131). Near the end of the notebook he was using at this time he added another long list of mechanical inventions and the following comment, which closely echoes Macaulay and antedates "A Majestic Literary Fossil" by nine years: "There is a difference between invention and application —The ancients invented; the modern spirit invents & applies." [7]

Another theme which plays an important role in the second part of *Life on the Mississippi* likewise can be found in the notes of 1880. Perhaps as a result of the extensive reading he was doing in southern materials for his encyclopedia of humor, Twain reasserted strongly his earlier identification of the South with feudalism by observing that "there is hardly a [written above: "not a single"] celebrated Southern name in any of the departments of human industry except those of war, murder [canceled: "assassination, lynching"], the duel, repudiation, & massacre." [8] This identification had already been made ten years before in a sketch called "The 'Tournament' in A.D. 1870," but it was held in abeyance in the 70's while Twain was exploiting his personal past from a very different point of view. Thus, although Tom Sawyer's swashbuckling fantasies clearly reflect the theme of southern feudalism, they are treated humorously and do not mar the village idyll. Actually the very year he published *Tom Sawyer* he wrote to a friend of his youth: "Ignorance, intolerance, egotism, self-assertion, opaque perception, dense and pitiful chuckle-headedness —and an almost pathetic unconsciousness of it all. That is

7. See above, pp. 29–32. Notebook references are to 14, p. 32; *Mark Twain's Notebook*, p. 156; and 15, p. 2, respectively.

8. Notebook 15, p. 7. A few pages earlier there is a long series of references to American humorists.

what I was at 19 and 20, and it is what the average Southerner is at 60 today" (*34*, 289). In short, Twain's attitudes toward both the region of his childhood and emergent industrial America which find their first significant expression in *Life on the Mississippi* were already well formed before his return to the river in 1882.

These attitudes were confirmed a thousandfold, however, not only by what he saw during his journey but also by his subsequent reading in the works of earlier southern travelers and adventurers. Clearly Twain came prepared to praise later nineteenth-century American civilization, and praise it he did in the second part of *Life on the Mississippi*. With some justice, John Q. Hays has written that "nowhere else did Twain so vociferously assert his modernity; nowhere else was he so full to the throat of the invention and satisfaction of his own time and country." [9] He was quick to note, for example, the changes in St. Louis—changes he said, "uniformly evidencing progress, energy, prosperity" (*12*, 193). As he traveled down the Mississippi, he described the improvements everywhere: new gadgets on the steamboats; plans for keeping the river in good condition; the factory towns of Helena and Memphis, with their growing populations and cotton receipts; new land companies that would establish equitable relations between the planter and the Negro; the marvelous ice factory and the expanding cotton mills at Natchez; finally New Orleans, "well outfitted with progressive men—thinking, sagacious, long-headed men," a city complete with a sewage system, electric lights, telephones, and new buildings (*12*, 341). All these improvements were but the beginning. "The signs are," he observed, "that the next twenty years will bring some noteworthy changes in the valley, in the direction of increased population and wealth and in the intellectual

9. "The Serious Elements in the Writing of Mark Twain" (diss., California, 1942), pp. 127–8.

advancement and the liberalizing of opinion which go naturally with these" (*12*, 303). From St. Louis northward Twain became even more enthusiastic, observing "all the enlivening signs of the presence of active, energetic, intelligent, prosperous, practical nineteenth-century populations." These people, he emphasized, "don't dream; they work" (*12*, 461).

Twain's derogatory use of the word "dream" indicates the degree to which he had, at least intellectually, repudiated the village society of his youth. In the passages quoted above, he decisively rejected the image of the "dreaming" society and embraced "civilization" in all its complexities —urbanization, wealth, growth of population, and (in this case) industrialism.[1] Historical development was welcomed and from it would come intellectual advancement. But would men be morally "better" because of this advancement? The burgeoning, energetic population of the upper Mississippi Valley Twain described as "an independent race who think of themselves, and who are competent to do it, because they are educated and enlightened; they keep

1. It should be noted that the fulsome praise of industrial America found in the published version of *Life on the Mississippi* was originally tempered by a chapter written for that book but later suppressed in which he listed those features of American life which the post-Civil War had accentuated: "bribery, jobbery, and general corruption"; or, more specifically, venal governing bodies, "tyrannical" capitalism, and lack of moral courage on the part of individual citizens (*Life on the Mississippi*, ed. Willis Wager, New York, The Heritage Press, 1933, pp. 407–11). These are the same subjects Twain had satirized in *The Gilded Age*. They loomed constantly larger as his disillusionment with the nineteenth century increased. Only one scene, however, in the published manuscript of *Life on the Mississippi* is reminiscent of the satire of the earlier book, the one in which two salesmen brag to each other about the fraudulent products their companies produce. Twain's comment is succinct and damning: "Brisk men," he called them, "energetic of movement and speech; the dollar their god, how to get it their religion" (*12*, 326)—a significant remark considering that, in his later writing, Twain is continually debating whether it is better to worship money (America, the present) or social position (Europe, the past).

abreast of the best and newest thought; they fortify every weak place in their land with a school, a college, a library, and a news-paper; and they live under law. Solicitude for the future of a race like this is not in order" (*12*, 469). To the crucial moral question Twain in the end ventured no direct answer. Instead he strongly repeated the Whig credo of law, education, and free institutions, and, by way of contrast, attempted to describe the barbarism of the America of his youth.

His original plan was to heighten what Willis Wager calls the "historical point of reference implicit in the entire book" by wide quotation from the early travelers to America: Mrs. Trollope, Dickens, C. A. Murray, Feardon, Marryat, Basil Hall, and probably others.[2] In a passage later suppressed Twain said that he "drudged through all those old books, mainly to find out what the procession of foreign tourists thought of the Mississippi." [3] He used them, in short, to establish points of comparison between the past and the present, and he defended them because they supported his thesis that earlier Americans were barbarians. In a passage omitted from the published text but highly revelatory of his own attitudes, Twain wrote, for example, of the much maligned Mrs. Trollope:

> She found a "civilization" here which you, reader, could not have endured; and which you would not have regarded as a civilization at all. Mrs. Trollope spoke of this civilization in plain terms . . . Her voice rises in indignation, sometimes but the object justifies the attitude—being slavery, rowdyism, "chivalrous" assassinations, sham godliness, and several other devilishnesses which would be as hateful to you, now,

2. *Life on the Mississippi* (Heritage ed.), p. 387.

3. Ibid., p. 411. Twain, like anyone else, was never without mixed motives. He was in a hurry to finish *Life on the Mississippi*, and quotations from these travelers—some 11,000 words—helped to fill out his text.

> as they were to her then. She was holily hated for her "prejudices," but they seem to have been simply the prejudices of a humane spirit against inhumanities . . . of a clean breeding against grossness . . . She found here a tissue-cuticled semi-barbarism which set itself up for a lofty civilization; and she skinned this thing and showed the world (and it) just what it was.

This was Twain's text, and he was quick to support it by chapter and verse. In biting phrases he reconstructed an earlier America. Cincinnati "with all its heart in pork and religion"; the blustering patriots who swaggered around "hand under coat-tails, hat tilted over left eye, spoiling for a fight"; the literature "almost wholly English—stolen mainly"; and everywhere religion and slavery, both of which a man must abide by "as solemnly as regularly as he does by his segar, his rum, and his business"—these are but a few examples of the general indictment which Twain concluded by saying:

> Such was the America which existed when this procession of foreign inspectors filed through the land, but which America has since passed away, leaving scarcely a vestige. We mourn, of course, as filial duty requires —yet it was good rotten material for burial.[4]

Such passages are indicative not only of the conscious historical assumptions behind much of Twain's best writing, but also of his specific artistic intentions in *Life on the Mississippi*. Certainly, in this work, the abundant statistical and topical information which De Lancey Ferguson once described as "having nothing to commend it save a faint historical boredom," is made more meaningful by a knowledge of what Twain was reacting against.[5] Had he elected

4. Ibid., pp. 392, 404–7.
5. *Mark Twain: Man and Legend* (New York, Bobbs-Merrill, 1943), p. 212.

to include his detailed discussion of early American travelers in the published book, his comments on progress would have seemed less a priori, his attitude toward Scott less arbitrary, and, in general, his theme and the entire purpose of the book would have been made immeasurably clearer.

Twain's attack on Scott, indeed, and the aristocratic (or "feudal" or "medieval") tradition for which Scott was a handy symbol is central to the meaning of *Life on the Mississippi*. We must not allow the arguments of those critics who have solemnly rebuked Twain for blaming all the South's troubles on Scott to blind us to the importance of his main contention: that the values represented by Scott were barbaric to begin with, hostile to the American liberal tradition, and totally incompatible with the new industrialism.[6] "Admiration of his fantastic heroes," Twain wrote,

6. The sharpest refutations have come from G. Harrison Orians, "Walter Scott, Mark Twain and the Civil War," *South Atlantic Quarterly, 40* (1941), 342–59; and V. R., "Walter Scott and the Southern States of America," *Notes and Queries, 169* (1935), 328–30. V. R. notes that George Borrow had a similar conception of Scott's role but misses a doubly ironic situation much closer home. Twain attacked Cooper as the American Scott, but Cooper himself felt that Scott was dangerous for the American reader because of his deference to hereditary rank, to "mere feudal and conventional laws, which have their origin in force, and are continued by prejudice and wrong" (*Gleanings in Europe: England,* New York, Oxford Univ. Press, 1930, *2,* 153). To compound the confusion further, modern criticism tends to stress that Scott, as a philosophical historian, was "the true successor to Hume and Robertson," a thoroughgoing believer in the progress of society (Alfred W. Benn, *History of English Rationalism in the 19th Century,* London, Longmans, Green, 1906, *1,* 310). See also Joseph E. Duncan, "The Anti-Romantic in *Ivanhoe,*" *Nineteenth-Century Fiction, 9* (1955), 293–300. For Scott's own sketch of the "progress of human society" see *Tales of a Grandfather: the History of Scotland* (Boston, 1861), *2,* 219–35. The ultimate cause of this confusion was the tension in Scott himself—not to mention in his readers and admirers—between a fascination (partly aesthetic) with the heroic past and an intellectual conviction of the moral superiority of his own time. This is the same tension which has been felt even more strongly by generations of American writers including Twain and which is central to *Life on the Mississippi.*

The continuing hostility of the South toward liberalism and industrializa-

> and their grotesque "chivalry" doings and romantic juvenilities still survives here in Baton Rouge in an atmosphere in which is already perceptible the wholesome and practical nineteenth-century smell of cotton factories and locomotives; and traces of its inflated language and other windy humbuggeries survive along with it.

The state capitol at Baton Rouge, a "little sham castle," was built, according to Twain, of "materials all ungenuine within and without, pretending to be what they are not," and it was a "hurtful thing and a mistake as a symbol and breeder and sustainer of maudlin Middle-Age romanticism here in the midst of the plainest and sturdiest and infinitely greatest and worthiest of all the centuries the world has seen" (*12*, 334). The values of Scott were a threat to democracy; they had checked the wave of progress from the French Revolution and "set the world in love with dreams and phantoms . . . with decayed and degraded systems of government, with the sillinesses and emptinesses, sham grandeurs, sham gauds . . . of a brainless and worthless long-vanished society." Finally, the romantic school of Scott had inhibited the growth of modern literature in the South. The authors, Twain complained, "write for the past, not the present; they use obsolete forms and a dead language" (*12*, 375–7). The southern aristocratic tradition, in short, with its antidemocratic tone, its economics that denied "practical common sense, progressive ideas, and progressive

---

tion is traced in H. N. Smith, "Minority Report: the Tradition of the Old South" in *Literary History of the United States,* ed. Spiller, Thorp, Johnson, and Canby (rev. ed., New York, 1953), pp. 607–17; in Louis D. Rubin, Jr., "The Historical Image of Modern Southern Writers," *Journal of Southern History, 22* (1956), 147–66; and in C. Vann Woodward, "The Historical Dimension," *Virginia Quarterly Review, 32* (1956), 358–67. These writers, incidentally, all point out that the sense of time and history so characteristic of southern writers is, to a great extent, the result of their intimate contact with two widely disparate cultural traditions. This may help explain Twain's interest in history.

works," its aesthetic and moral sham, represented a compendium of the qualities in earlier America, especially the America of the southern frontier, to which Twain was reacting most violently when he chanted his song of progress in *Life on the Mississippi*.

But Twain was not content merely to attack feudalism in its later manifestations. Though he eventually omitted descriptions of Mrs. Trollope's America, he used material borrowed from Parkman to form at least a rudimentary historical frame for the entire book, and plunged his theme of progress far back in time by delivering a savage assault directly on the Middle Ages. When DeSoto first saw the river, for instance,

> the absurd chivalry business was in full feather, and the joust and the tournament were the frequent pastime of titled fine gentlemen who could fight better than they could spell while religion was the passion of their ladies, and the classifying their offspring into children of full rank and children by brevet their pastime. In fact, all around, religion was in a peculiarly blooming condition . . . the Spanish Inquisition was roasting, and racking, and burning, with a free hand; elsewhere on the Continent the nations were being persuaded to holy living by the Sword and Fire. [*12*, 6]

Ignorance, sexual immorality, a cruel and hypocritical religion—the counts in Twain's indictment of the Middle Ages in these chapters show a clear thematic link between the growing disenchantment of his European tour of 1878–79 and *A Connecticut Yankee* of ten years later.

But if, on the one hand, *Life on the Mississippi* anticipates *A Connecticut Yankee* and its doctrine of salvation by ameliorating social institutions, on the other it echoes the central theme of *Huckleberry Finn:* the dream of man as innately innocent and without need of salvation; the rejection of institutions which do not redeem but corrupt. The Yankee, for all his intrepid force and vigor, is representative of a civilization, a figure in time and history; Huck is essentially mythic, larger than his temporal manifestations and beyond history. The Yankee remains Twain's most heroic attempt to embrace history; Huck, his first and most successful effort to escape its futility. The seeds of both these figures and of the meaning Twain attaches to them can be found in *Life on the Mississippi.*

It is quickly apparent, in the first place, that in *Life on the Mississippi* the historical rhythm of the river itself is by no means identical with the rhythm of the civilization on its banks. The river towns move steadily from torpor to bustling development. The Mississippi, however, moves from torpor to activity and back to a state not far different from its virginal tranquillity. Thus in his account of the organization of his book it is actually the historical rhythm of the river that Twain describes when he says that he will "glance briefly at its [the river's] slumbrous first epoch in a couple of short chapters; at its second and wide awake epoch in a couple more; at its flushest and widest-awake epoch in a good many succeeding chapters; and then talk about its comparatively tranquil present epoch in what shall be left of the book" (*12*, 4–5). In other words, the "flush times" on the Mississippi occurred while the society of the valley itself was still (to use Twain's metaphor) "slumbering." As a result of his hardened attitude toward earlier America, Twain found himself, in the 1880's, in the position of celebrating the past of the river itself while at the same time he was damning the civilization which had surrounded it.

In *Life on the Mississippi* the tensions and ambiguities of this situation are everywhere felt and center especially about Twain's use of the word "romance"; for while he was asserting that the "sham" romance of the aristocratic tradition was "good rotten material for burial," he was ceaselessly lamenting that "the romance of the river was gone." Since in both instances the reference is to the same historical period, we can only resolve the paradox by assigning in each case a different set of values to the word "romance." [7] When used in connection with the society on the banks of the river, it stood (as we have already noted) for all those feudal customs and conventions that were inimical to plain, prosaic, democratic, and morally decent nineteenth-century America. When, on the other hand, it was used in connection with life on the river itself, true romance meant for Twain the independent struggle by a strong and capable individual against the forces that control human existence. It meant, in a word, adventure—heroic not in its moral purity but in its grandiosity, its feats of skill and daring, and, above all, its freedom. True romance was the antithesis and eternal enemy of the false as Huck was antithetical (and potentially hostile) to Tom Sawyer. True romance was the celebration of the American folk hero; false romance was the perpetuation of a foreign mythology on an alien soil.

History had brought "progress," of course, on the river just as it had on land, but on the river it had crushed out certain values for which Twain could not help mourning. Gone was the personality both functional and colorful (as opposed to the "sham" knight of the aristocratic tradition). Uncle Mumford, for instance, the steamboat mate with thirty years' experience on the Mississippi, Twain described as a man with strong opinions, much experience, and

> just a perceptible dash of poetry in his composition, an easy gift of speech, a thick growl in his voice, and an oath or two where he can get at them when the ex-

7. Critics from De Voto to Gladys Bellamy and Dixon Wecter have missed the point by going through the book cataloguing its "romantic" and "realistic" elements—and, in the process, introducing their own definition of romance (usually the exclusion of base and sordid subject matter).

> igencies of his office require a spiritual lift. He is a mate of the blessed old-time kind; and goes d- - -ing around . . . in a way to mellow the ex-steamboatman's heart with sweet, soft longings for the vanished days that shall come no more. [*12*, 210]

Mumford's dress was as vivid as his personality, as appropriate to the wild and free spirit which made him so different from the standardized and institutionally produced men characteristic of the nineteenth century. He was, Twain adds, "still in the slouch garb of the old generation of mates; but next trip the Anchor line will have him in uniform—a natty blue naval uniform, with brass buttons, along with all the officers of the line—and then he will be a totally different style of scenery from what he is now." Up to this point, Twain seems to be singing the familiar requiem for a vanished past so commonplace in modern literature. But he continues:

> Uniforms on the Mississippi! It beats all other changes put together, for surprise. Still, there is another surprise—that it was not made fifty years ago. It is so manifestly sensible that it might have been thought of earlier one would suppose. During fifty years out there, the innocent passenger in need of help and information has been mistaking the mate for the cook, and the captain for the barber—and being roughly entertained for it, too. But his troubles are ended now. And the greatly improved aspect of the boat's staff is another advantage achieved by the dress uniform. [*12*, 210–11]

Collateral with longings for the past of the river (as distinct from the past of the society on its banks) is the complete acceptance of the forces that have brought about its destruction.

All Twain's descriptions of rivermen take on an archetypal quality. This fact is perhaps not so evident in his treatment of Uncle Mumford as it is in his description of the mate he meets on the *Paul Jones* as a small boy. This man was "huge and muscular, his face . . . bearded and whiskered all over . . . and in the matter of profanity sublime . . . When he gave even the simplest order, he discharged it like a blast of lightning, and sent a long, reverberating peal of profanity thundering after it" (*12*, 40–1). His size, his profanity, the lightning image all proclaim his kinship with the "comic demi-gods" of the river.

At the very center of this archetype were the raftsmen. It was when commenting on this particular type of river personality that Twain depicted most explicitly the change he had already noted among the deck officers of the steamboats. The sight of modern lumber rafts on the Upper Mississippi "shoved swiftly along by a powerful sternwheeler" and manned by "small crews" of "quiet, orderly men, of a sedate business aspect, with not a suggestion of romance about them anywhere" recalled to him the rafts of his youth, "floating leisurely along . . . manned with joyous and reckless crews of fiddling, song-singing, whiskey-drinking, break-down-dancing rapscallions" (*12*, 476). In this case, the antipodal sets of values around which the materials of *Life on the Mississippi* are organized lie in particularly sharp juxtaposition: on the one hand, law-abiding, efficient, prosaic crewmen, who were so completely a part of the Industrial Revolution that they seemed scarcely more than an extension of the machine they ostensibly controlled; on the other, the happy and free "old-fashioned" boatmen, who were "the sublimates of frontier hardness," [8]

8. As De Voto describes them in *Mark Twain's America* (Boston, Little, Brown, 1932), p. 60. For a good review (using Rourke, De Voto, and Parrington) of the historical aspects of the folk legends which lie behind Twain's conception of the romance of the river, see *Half Horse Half Alligator: The Growth of the Mike Fink Legend*, eds. Walter Blair and Franklin J. Meine (Chicago, 1956), pp. 31–3.

the prototypes of that anarchic individualism (that repudiation of *all* institutions, European and American) which, in the American experience, has served as counterpoise to the dream of progress through enlightened civilization.

Still more important are the connotations of boyish high spirits and good nature—even a certain kind of innocence—that cling to Twain's depiction of the river men. They lacked meanness and hypocrisy; while violating every legal and moral code of the society from which they were outcasts, they nevertheless (perhaps *because* of their rebellion—the ambiguity here is crucial) possessed certain fundamental virtues. As he described them elsewhere in *Life on the Mississippi,* the river men were

> rough and hardy . . . rude, uneducated, brave, suffering terrific hardships with sailor-like stoicism; heavy drinkers, coarse frolickers in moral sties like the Natchez-under-the-hill of that day, heavy fighters, reckless fellows, every one, elephantinely jolly, foul-witted, profane, prodigal of their money, bankrupt at the end of the trip, fond of barbaric finery, prodigious braggarts; yet, in the main, honest, trustworthy, faithful to promises and duty, and often picturesquely magnanimous. [*12*, 18]

Unmodified by either middle-class respectability or the code of romantic feudalism, the ingenuousness of the river men was at once innate, childlike, and monumental.

Even the heartless villains among them possessed a fabulous quality, a kind of heroic stature, that raised them, in a sense, beyond good and evil—that gave them a kind of independent value beyond mundane moral judgments. Thus Twain could contrast the "old-fashioned" river pirate Murel with Jesse James in much the same way he had contrasted the old and new boatman. Murel, he said, was James' equal

> in boldness, in pluck, in rapacity; in cruelty, brutality, heartlessness, treachery, and in general and comprehensive vileness and shamelessness; and very much his superior in some larger aspects. James was a retail rascal; Murel, wholesale . . . What are James and his half-dozen vulgar rascals compared with this stately old-time criminal, with his sermons, his meditated insurrections and city-captures, and his majestic following of ten hundred men, sworn to do his evil will.
> [*12*, 243]

Twain enjoyed using the word "vulgar" in its basic meaning of low, plebeian, common (i.e. opposed to everything noble) to describe modern conditions. The "noble science of piloting," for example, was destroyed when "some genius . . . introduced the plan of towing a dozen steamer cargoes down to New Orleans at the tail of a vulgar little tugboat" (*12*, 142). Murel was evil but not vulgar; rather, he is almost redeemed by his grandiosity.

It was in the figure of the pilot, however, the chief of the river hierarchy, that Twain's conception of true romance found its apotheosis. He was independence incarnate. Upon the pilot (and, through the pilot, upon the lesser denizens of the river), Twain projected the sense of psychological release which he himself must have felt during his years on the Mississippi. "I loved the profession far better than any I have followed since," he wrote in *Life on the Mississippi,* "and I took a measureless pride in it. The reason is plain: a pilot, in those days, was the only unfettered and entirely independent human being that lived on the earth." He went on to say that kings, parliaments, newspaper editors, clergymen, writers ("we 'modify' before we print") were all the "manacled servants" of the institutions they allegedly led. And he concluded: "In truth, every man and woman and child has a master, and worries and frets in servitude; but in the day I write of, the Mississippi pilot had none" (*12*, 118–19). Again it is the uniqueness of the river experience that Twain stressed, its freedom from the enveloping determinism, the moral failure (men struggling, or at least longing, for independence in situations which are beyond their will to control), the ultimate cowardice of life in a civilized community—indeed, of life anywhere but on the river itself.

At the same time, the pilot was a man of merciless empiricism and superb technical precision. The young boy who runs away to become a pilot in the opening chapters of *Life on the Mississippi* dreams of glorious and blood-curdling adventures in "mysterious lands and distant climes," but he gradually learns of the terrible dangers close at hand on the river itself and the hard work, skill, and mastery of details required to overcome them. As his initiation deepens, his fantasy world more and more falls away.[9] In the end the boy can read the "wonderful book" of the river—"there never was so wonderful a book written by man"—and can act firmly, daringly when necessary, on the evidence supplied by his reading. The picturesque surface of the book, however, is no longer part of his vision: "I had lost something which could never be restored to me while I lived. All the grace, the beauty, the poetry, had gone out of the majestic river!" Underneath the dimpled waters covered with "all manner of pretty pictures . . . painted by the sun and shaded by the clouds" lurked the wreck or rock "that could tear the life out of the strongest vessel that ever floated" (*12*, 77–80). In the complex set of values which Twain associated with piloting there was pro-

9. E.g. after getting up at night to go to work in the pilot-house: "I began to fear that piloting was not quite so romantic as I had imagined it was; there was something very real and work-like about this new phase of it" (*12*, 47).

vision not only for heroic action but for realism and honesty.

Modern society, of course, with its peculiar penchant for efficiency, had destroyed even this "race apart and not like the other folk" (*35*, 542). The fate of Mumford and the raftsmen had overtaken the pilot; he had become simply another servant of the machine and completely "like other folk." Describing the process half seriously, half comically, Twain noted:

> In these new days of infinite change, the Anchor Line have raised the captain above the pilot by giving him the bigger wages of the two. This was going far, but they have not stopped there . . . We that were once the aristocrats of the River, can't go to bed now, as we used to do, and sleep while a hundred tons of freight are lugged aboard; no, we must sit in the pilot-house and keep awake too. Verily we are being treated like a parcel of mates and engineers. The government has taken away the romance of our calling; the Company has taken away its state and dignity.

The government's contribution to the debasement of the pilot, as Twain described it in an earlier paragraph, was to place lamps at the head of every crossing and to tear snags out of the river with patrol boats (*12*, 231–4). With these innovations (reluctantly approved by Twain), the heroic adventurer became a functionary in a mechanized system. True romance, in short, had disappeared from the world with the river men, leaving behind it only a dream —but a dream that Twain was to shape into his greatest image of power, freedom, and beauty. During the decade in which he most completely embraced the progressivist position, he was also drawn strongly to a set of values which were profoundly antithetical, not only to progress but to the very process of history itself as he defined it. *Life on the Mississippi,* in effect, points in two directions, and these are the directions Twain pursued in *Huckleberry Finn* and *A Connecticut Yankee.*

Certainly the *Yankee* can be most meaningfully read as a serious attempt by Twain to embody the theme of historical progress in a major novel. In the following chapter we shall first describe the immediate intellectual background of the book and then examine specifically the ways in which Twain articulates his theme. Finally, we shall note how the ultimate fate of his Promethean hero adds an unexpected dimension to this curious and complex book.

6.

THE FALL OF PROMETHEUS: *A Connecticut Yankee*

> Intrepid, unprincipled, reckless, predatory, with boundless ambition, civilized in externals but a savage at heart, America is, or may yet be the Paul Jones of nations.
>
> Melville, *Israel Potter*

If all history were somehow corrupting, then goodness and independence could be found only among those who had escaped history by flight from society, extreme youth, some kind of miraculous intervention (e.g. Joan of Arc), or by some combination of these methods. If, on the other hand, only the institutions of certain historical epochs were corrupting, then goodness and independence could be found among all those whose characters had been shaped during other epochs by institutions which inculcated these desired ideals. In other words, man was either born innately good and made bad, or he was born innately bad (or not good enough so that life in history was superfluous) and—at least under certain conditions—trained to be much better. Between these two propositions Twain wavers in his writing, pulled first in one direction, then in another as his reading in history and the direct experience of the moment seemed to dictate. In the later

1880's the two most important influences on his mind were undoubtedly Matthew Arnold and William Hartpole Lecky.

Twain's controversy with Arnold has been noted on several occasions by critics.[1] Neither man, for obvious reasons, was able to understand what the other was talking about. Twain's work, according to Arnold, was the exact expression of "the more gay and light type" of Philistine; [2] for Twain, "Matthew Arnold's civilization . . . was *superficial polish*." [3] Beneath a good deal of personal acrimony, what was basically at issue was Arnold's contention that Americans were a hard, practical, materialistic people—that in America there was little to "nourish and delight the sense of beauty." There were no cathedrals, no homes of the great to create in Americans a sense of distinction. Americans, in short, needed to feel the "discipline of awe and respect." At the same time, Arnold praised American social and political equality (though he attacked the "absence of truth and soberness" in our newspapers) and acknowledged that such equality was ahead of similar developments in England; but he insisted that political and material achievements did not in themselves constitute an adequate definition of civilization.[4]

Twain, however, argued that they did because they led to general moral development. Ignoring the fact that Arnold wanted to cultivate rather than abolish the middle classes, Twain attempted time and again during the late

1. See especially John B. Hoben, "Mark Twain's *A Connecticut Yankee:* A Genetic Study," *American Literature, 18* (1946), 197–218, and D. M. McKeithan, "More about Mark Twain's War with English Critics of America," *Modern Language Notes, 63* (1948), 221–8. McKeithan is, of course, right in stressing that Arnold's comments on America merely hardened attitudes already held by Twain and caused him in the *Yankee* to extend his satire so that it embraced modern England. He notes, as I have, that Twain had attacked feudalism long before the 80's.

2. *Civilization in the United States* (Boston, 1900), p. 93.

3. Notebook 22(II) (1887–88), p. 64. Italics are Twain's.

4. Arnold, pp. 169–78.

80's to describe how his definition of civilization differed from that of the Englishman. "To me," he wrote in one essay, "it represents the stage which a whole people, not a class has reached, in well being & in mental & moral advancement. To me, a great civilization is one in which the mass of a [canceled: "people"] nation have reached a general higher level in these particulars; to Mr. Matthew Arnold it meant one in which the select few had reached a lofty moral and intellectual level." [5] What distinguished American civilization, what made it "the greatest & the best that exists in the earth—that ever has existed in the earth" was simply that "every man is a man," in other words, the complete political, social and moral freedom of Americans. Irreverence was not an unfortunate outgrowth but both a cause and a valuable result of this freedom and, in any case, inseparable from it. "To my mind," he said in an article defending the American press, "a discriminating irreverence is the creator and protector of human liberty —even as the other thing [i.e. solemnity and respect] is the creator and protector of all forms of human slavery, bodily and mental." [6]

Twain's controversy with Arnold thus deepened as well as hardened his nationalism. He was forced to define and analyze more closely than he had ever done before those basic ethical attitudes which he most cherished and locate them, so to speak, firmly planted on the margin of the river rather than on a raft floating downstream. That Twain should focus on the issue of irreverence is not surprising, for, in the context of his deterministic system, it represented the apex of human development—as radical a dream in its own way as that of man in Eden. The irreverent individual, indeed, was one who had transcended the society which produced him and thus was "free"; he had transcended it, however, not by the preservation of

5. "On Progress, Civilization, Monarchy, etc.," pp. 5–6.
6. "The American Press," quoted in Hoben, p. 209.

certain innate qualities through flight from institutions, but by being trained to challenge continually and call in question the very institutions which trained him. Thus, paradoxically, certain deterministic influences could produce an "independent" man. His own aim in writing *A Connecticut Yankee,* Twain noted at the time of its composition, was to teach *disloyalty* to the nineteenth century "till they get used to disusing that word *loyalty* as representing a virtue. This will beget independence—which is loyalty to one's best self and principles, and this is often disloyalty to the general idols and fetishes." [7]

But if it was Arnold who goaded Twain into a more complete formulation of his ideas concerning man in society, it was Lecky's *History of European Morals* which gave these ideas, for the first time, a substantial historical foundation. All his life, as we have noted repeatedly, Twain himself had attempted to link morality and history, but his conclusions necessarily had been limited to the more obvious: the sexual immorality and barbarism of feudalism, its cruel legal and social code, the sham of false romanticism. Lecky's broad analysis of the ethical bases of classical and medieval civilization added an entirely new dimension to Twain's ideas and gave them a systematic form while, at the same time, furnishing materials that were immediately applicable to the controversy with Arnold. One key passage from Lecky, marked by Twain in his copy of the book, is so important to an understanding of *A Connecticut Yankee* that it deserves quotation in some detail. In it, Lecky directly contrasts Christian with pagan morality:

> In active benevolence, in the spirit of reverence, in loyalty, in co-operative habits, they [the Middle Ages]

7. Notebook 23(I) (1888), p. 17, published in *Mark Twain's Notebook,* p. 199. Italics are Twain's.

> far transcend the noblest ages of Pagan antiquity . . . On the other hand they rank immeasurably below the best Pagan civilizations in civic and patriotic virtues, in the love of liberty . . . in the dignity and beauty of the type of character they formed. They had their full share of tumult, anarchy, injustice, and war, and they should probably be placed, in all intellectual virtues, lower than any other period in the history of mankind. A boundless intolerance of all divergence of opinion was united with an equally boundless toleration of all falsehood. . . . Credulity being taught as a virtue, and all conclusions dictated by authority, a deadly torpor sank upon the human mind, which for many centuries almost suspended its action, and was only effectively broken by the . . . free thinking habits that accompanied the rise of the industrial republics in Italy. Few men who are not either priests or monks would not have preferred to live in the best days of the Athenian or of the Roman republics . . . rather than in any period that elapsed between the triumph of Christianity and the fourteenth century.

Lecky's description in these lines of the sense of reverence, obedience, and submissiveness of the medieval Christian is made even more explicit in his extended discussion of slavery. Here his main point is that Christianity "imparted a moral dignity to the servile classes, and . . . gave an unexampled impetus to the movement of enfranchisement," but it did all this essentially by giving "the servile virtues the foremost place in the moral type." Lecky goes on to note that "magnanimity, self-reliance, dignity, independence, and, in a word, elevation of character, constituted the Roman ideal of perfection" whereas "humility, obedience, gentleness, patience, resignation, are all cardinal or rudimentary virtues in the Christian character." Twain's sympathetic response to this hypothesis is clear enough from a marginal comment: "Christianity then did not raise up the slave, but degraded all conditions of men to the slave's level." [8]

For all his obvious bias as a spokesman for the Whig-Liberal position, Lecky, as a professional historian, was required to maintain a standard of objectivity which Twain felt no compulsion to imitate. Nevertheless, *A Connecticut Yankee* is essentially a crude and fictionalized reformulation of Lecky's ideas. In the *Yankee,* indeed, is the same radical bifurcation of Western history described in much the same terms of Roman Church versus secular (and preferably democratic) state, religion versus science, slavery versus freedom, obedience versus independence. That Twain contrasts the Dark Ages with the nineteenth century rather than with pagan antiquity does not, of course, introduce a new and complicating third factor into Lecky's scheme. Like many other thinkers of the eighteenth and nineteenth century, both men posited a more or less golden age of Greece and Rome, which was destroyed eventually by "barbarism and Christianity," only to rise again, this time for good, under the aegis of the new scientific thought in the eighteenth century. The Dark

8. *History of European Morals from Augustus to Charlemagne* (New York, 1955), pp. 15–16, 66–8. For a description of Twain's various marginal notations in Lecky see "Mark Twain's Religious Beliefs as Indicated by Notations in His Books," *The Twainian, 9,* Nos. 3, 4, 5, 6 (May—December 1955), 1–4, 1–4, 1–4, 3–4. The pagination of my edition is slightly different from that which Twain was using and to which the editors of *The Twainian* allude. Paine claims that Twain was reading the *History of European Morals* (published 1869) as early as 1873. According to the editors of *The Twainian,* the marked copy of Lecky in their possession has the date 1906 on the fly-leaf. This obviously is not the first time Twain read the *History,* however, since in both the actual text of the *Yankee* and in notebook references he points out that he took the St. Simon Stylites material from Lecky's book. In any case, its influence on his thought first becomes marked in the 80's.

Ages were a "break in continuity," a "lapse" (as the eighteenth century tried to explain it) in the relentless forward march of history—what Twain called a "moral and mental midnight," from which man awoke into the Enlightenment and the great nineteenth century, the latter almost entirely responsible for "the valuable part . . . of what we call civilization" (*36,* 208). Almost all Twain's reading would have caused him to divide Western history into two camps in this fashion; Lecky's influence on the *Yankee* is apparent simply in the completeness and explicitness of the division and the terms in which it is described.

The villain of the book is clearly the Church. Behind the barbarism, behind the absurd social code of feudalism lurked (in the Yankee's words)

> the hand of that awful power the Roman Catholic Church. In two or three little centuries it had converted a nation of men to a nation of worms. Before the day of the Church's supremacy in the world, men were men, and held their heads up, and had a man's pride and spirit and independence; and what of greatness and position a person got, he got mainly by achievement, not by birth. But then the Church came to the front . . . she invented "divine right of things," and propped it all around, brick by brick, with the Beatitudes . . . she preached (to the commoner) meekness under insult; preached (still to the commoner, always to the commoner) patience, meanness of spirit, non-resistance under oppression; and she introduced heritable ranks and aristocracies, and taught all the Christian population of the earth to bow down to them and worship them. Even down to my birth-century that poison was still in the blood of Christendom . . . Of course that taint, that reverence for rank and title, had been in our American blood,

> too—I know that; but when I left America it had disappeared—at least to all intents and purposes. [*14*, 64–5]

This is Twain's most comprehensive discussion of the role of the Catholic Church and the passage where the echo of Lecky is most clearly heard, but the general topic is broached again and again in the *Yankee.* It should be observed, moreover, that Twain does not limit his remarks to Catholicism. On one occasion, for example, the Boss points out that he had the power to make everyone a Presbyterian (his own sect), but he did not because he "was afraid of a united church; it makes a mighty power, the mightiest conceivable, and then when it by and by gets into selfish hands, as it always bound to do, it means death to human liberty and paralysis to human thought" (*14*, 77, 160). The eighteenth-century liberal image of the Roman Catholic Church became, in effect, Twain's general image of totalitarianism, what the monolithic state is to Orwell and other contemporary writers. Thus the absurdity of his later fantasy of Mary Baker Eddy as an American Pope should not blind us to the essential seriousness of his interpretation of the drift of history.

In the light of Twain's heavy debt to Lecky, it is clearly a mistake to consider *A Connecticut Yankee,* as many critics have done, merely as an attack on the English and Victorian England (which was, indeed, one of Twain's motives in writing the book) or as an indirect assault on industrial abuses and social injustice in general or even simply as a realistic appraisal of a way of life glorified by Scott and Tennyson. Actually, the *Yankee* is an interpretation of Western history since the fall of Rome presented in the familiar terms of contrasting civilizations. This idea of contrast in the novel Twain emphasized as early as 1886 in a letter to Mrs. Fairbanks. Because it was written to a highly respectable lady or because Twain himself was not yet fully aware of the more serious implications of such a juxtaposition of civilizations, this letter, to be sure, gives little hint of what the tone of the final book would be. Indeed, it stresses that Malory's "great and beautiful characters" will be left "unsmirched and unbelittled"—a statement which, while basically true, fails to suggest how these characters were going to look divested of their romantic trappings. But it clearly states the purpose of *A Connecticut Yankee* as Twain conceived it then and afterwards: to describe the Middle Ages as they would have appeared to an honest and rational observer and contrast them with the nineteenth century.[9]

All Twain's statements of intention regarding the *Yankee* (and he made them on numerous occasions) at least imply—when they do not strongly emphasize—this element of contrast. Even late in life recollecting the book, Twain described his literary aim as an attempt "to contrast . . . the English life of the whole of the Middle Ages, with the life of modern Christendom and modern civilization—to the advantage of the latter, of course." [1] Written just before the full flood of Utopian novels in the 1890's, *A Connecticut Yankee* actually reversed their procedure; where the Utopian novelist traditionally assumes that the society in which he lives is bad and attempts to describe a better one, Twain, on the other hand, described an immeasurably worse society in the past from a point in time in which those social reforms he felt most necessary had presumably been in large part achieved. "If any are inclined to rail at our present civilization," he suggested to his readers in an unpublished preface, "why—there is no hindering him, but he ought to sometimes contrast it with what went before and take comfort and hope, too." [2]

9. *Mark Twain to Mrs. Fairbanks,* pp. 257–8.
1. *Mark Twain in Eruption,* p. 211.
2. "Two Unused Prefaces to *A Connecticut Yankee,*" Paine 91, quoted in Hoben, p. 215.

Twain could hardly have stated the official theme of *A Connecticut Yankee* more explicitly. Eighteen eighty-nine, we must remember, is the year in which Twain wrote of both England and America: "These two civilizations have risen out of primeval night and they rest upon the horizon. Could they stop there if they would—with the zenith inviting them and the law of their inspiring march impelling them to seek it and achieve it?" [3]

The meaning of human experience, unfortunately, has a disconcerting tendency to vary according to one's angle of vision. The points of view of the novelist and of the philosophical historian are by no means similar, nor do they necessarily lead to compatible conclusions about life —even when the two roles are played concurrently by the same individual. In his illuminating little book *The Hedgehog and the Fox,* Isaiah Berlin points out that while Tolstoy was attacking the illusions of free choice in public life, he was, at the same time, extolling the virtues of private life with its sense of responsibility and freedom. In other words, "his genius lay in the perception of specific properties . . . Nevertheless he longed for a universal explanatory principle." This longing, in turn, sprang from "a bitter inner conflict between his actual experience and his beliefs, between his vision of life, and his theory of what it . . . ought to be, if the vision was to be bearable at all." A similar conflict is behind all the ambiguities of *A Connecticut Yankee.* Berlin goes on to compare Joseph de Maistre and Tolstoy in terms that are almost equally applicable to Twain: both were *au fond* unyieldingly pessimistic thinkers; yet "both sought some escape from their own inescapable and unanswerable scepticism in some vast impregnable truth which would protect them from the effects of their own natural inclinations and tempera-

3. See above, p. 28.

ment."[4] Try as they might, however, neither Twain nor Tolstoy was able to coerce his personal (novelist's) vision into conformity with his philosophical presuppositions. *A Connecticut Yankee* and *War and Peace* remain the products of a divided artistic consciousness, and in their imperfections show the perils of such a division. Indeed, *War and Peace* is successful as a novel only because Tolstoy creates a world so vivid, particularized, and complex that it finally renders irrelevant all his attempts at logical reduction. Twain was by no means so fortunate; the standoff battle between vision and theory in the *Yankee* turns the book into a shambles of discordant elements.

Obviously a novelist cannot rest content with abstractions. In developing fictionally his theme of progress, Twain was forced to deal with specific characters in concrete situations. How could he project dramatically the contrast between the Catholic Dark Ages and modern democratic and technological civilization? For a number of reasons, the structure of the travel book must have suggested itself to him in the period following his initial conception of the *Yankee* as a humorous dream fantasy. The loose episodic narrative is, in the first place, the general pattern of most of his fiction—an aspect of Twain's realism, his desire to imitate life closely in his fiction. In a note of around the time when he was beginning the *Yankee* he wrote: "What is biography? Unadorned romance. What is romance? Adorned biography. Adorn it less & it will be better than it is. A *narrative* novel is the thing, perhaps: where you follow the fortunes of two or three people & have no plot more than real life has."[5] Moreover, the characteristic literary formula by which Twain develops his social criticism is that of the traveler between cultures: the young American journeying to Europe and the Near

4. New York, Simon and Schuster (1953), pp. 27–36, 59.
5. Notebook 21, p. 9.

East where feudal traditions continue or exist vestigially in manners and artifacts; the rebellious Southerner returning South where these traditions had staged their most notable invasion of America; and, finally, the Yankee moving back through historical time to the heyday of feudalism. In every case, the traveler embodies a distinct set of values that he uses as a touchstone to measure the cultures with which he comes in contact. This is the formula used imaginatively to good satiric effect in the eighteenth century (when, for the first time, men became sharply aware of differences in institutions) and—what is more relevant to our purposes—in the nineteenth century by the succession of European, British, and American travelers who found endless fascination in analyzing each other's homelands. Twain, of course, began his career as a newspaper correspondent, and the pattern of his first book, *The Innocents Abroad,* dominates much of his later work. His notebooks are filled with plans for imaginary journeys which echo both the satiric essay of the eighteenth century (e.g. "To satirize the world in petto—write private journal of a Pitcairn Islander") and the nineteenth century travel book (e.g. "Write an Englishman's Tour in America").[6]

In *A Connecticut Yankee* Twain depended heavily on the travel motif, not only because he found it a congenial way in which to organize literary materials, but also because it was a familiar device of medieval romance. The Yankee's humorous and brutally realistic account of his journeys is a devastating travesty of Malory's legendary and imaginative accounts of knightly pilgrimages and, as such, tends to make the entire romantic tradition seem ludicrous and the values associated with that tradition empty, false, and vicious.[7] Twain went out of his way to make his book

6. Notebook 15, p. 59, and 12, p. 11, respectively.

7. For a detailed description of the skillful manner in which Twain

seem literally the story of a journey into the Middle Ages by someone who travels extensively while there and incorporates his experiences and impressions into a manuscript. In every possible way the fanciful elements of the dream convention are eschewed in favor of actual events which affect body as well as mind. The Yankee himself describes the phenomenon that has transformed his life, not as a dream, but as a "transposition of epochs—and bodies" similar to the transmigration of souls (*14*, 2). He is knocked out in Hartford at the age of thirty-two and found eight years later by the author a broken and dying man wandering through the halls of Warwick Castle, his speech full of medievalisms and his smile "not a modern smile, but one that must have gone out of general use many, many centuries ago" (*14*, 2). His adventures, furthermore, are given a certain empiric validity by the bullet hole which Twain observes in the hauberk of Sir Sagramor le Desirous that hangs in Warwick Castle. Obviously, like Jonathan Swift in *Gulliver's Travels,* Twain consciously attempted to stress the reality of the adventures of his hero, and, in so doing fell into the familiar pattern of the travel book.

There is at least one other resemblance between *A Connecticut Yankee* and *Gulliver's Travels*: in both books there is a constant shifting of point of view because there is a constant fluctuation in the relationship of the author to his main character. Sometimes they are virtually synonymous; sometimes they are widely divergent from one another. In *Gulliver's Travels,* however, point of view is consciously manipulated to create an artistically valid ambiguity which heightens and extends the dramatic force of the theme; at the same time, the moral center of the book remains relatively stable. In *A Connecticut Yankee,*

---

uses material and devices found in Malory as a weapon against the whole tradition see Robert H. Wilson, "Malory in the *Connecticut Yankee,*" *Univ. of Texas Studies in English,* 27 (1948), 145–206.

on the other hand, point of view unconsciously wavers and leads to confusion of meaning because of the fundamental disparity between Twain's predominantly optimistic theory of history and his personal pessimism. This disparity is reflected in the split personality of the Yankee. As traveler, observer, theorist he is a direct and unabashed spokesman for Twain; as a consciously contrived literary character deeply involved in his own personal ambitions and conflicts, he is someone whom Twain keeps at arm's length and eventually destroys. As spokesman, he is an advocate of progress; as character, he is a tragic victim of its illusions; and in neither role, is he treated with the irony that might have bridged the dualism. In the figure of Huckleberry Finn, on the contrary, there is no such split. Since Huck's strength is in his innate humanity rather than his rationality, he is a stable counterpoise to the society he is observing. Both his empirical observations (on the whole) and the fundamental values he himself stands for represent Twain's deepest convictions; and his moral, theological, and social beliefs—the impact of social convention on him—can be treated with appropriate irony.

Perhaps it is more correct to say, therefore, that the greater part of *A Connecticut Yankee* conforms to the structure of the travel book. The traveler is the Yankee, but he clearly speaks for Twain and Lecky as he moves boldly and confidently into the heart of medieval darkness. The Yankee's journey through England is, indeed, a searching exploration of the psychological results of long tyranny upon the human mind, of reverence forced but not earned. The English, he notes, "had been heritors and subjects of cruelty and outrage so long that nothing could have startled them but a kindness. . . . Their entire being was reduced to a monotonous dead level of patience, resignation, dumb uncomplaining acceptance of whatever might befall them in this life. Their very imagination was dead. When you can say that of a man, he has struck bottom" (*14*, 170). Because of Twain's southern background and his recent reading of Lecky, physical slavery is the compelling symbol of this degradation, and he wrings from it every ounce of emotional impact and intellectual significance. The horrors of the unhistorical but emotionally compelling death march through England of the gang of slaves which the Yankee and the King have to join against their will are described in meticulous detail: the endless walking and sleeping in irons that "had chafed the skin from their ankles and made sores which were ulcerated and wormy"; the faces "gray with a coating of dust . . . like . . . the coating upon furniture in unoccupied houses"; the trader with his whip "with a short handle and long lash divided into several knotted tails"; and, finally, the oversentimentalized but still powerful picture of the young mother mercilessly beaten and then sold apart from her husband. But cruelty, however terrible, is not the worst effect of slavery; ironically, it saves its most devastating punishment for those who are not slaves by "ossifying what one may call the superior lobe of human feeling" (*14*, 186–90).[8] Thus on one occasion in *A Connecticut Yankee* the slave gang sits with bowed heads in the public square of Cambenet while "by hideous contrast, a redundant orator was making a speech to another gathering not thirty steps away, in fulsome laudation of 'our glorious British liberties.' " This final phrase is reminiscent of Bernard Shaw; Twain at the same time makes his ironic point and gives the Lion's tail a vicious twist (*14*, 349).

Twain gives wider application to this master-slave relationship with all its attendant evils by applying it to the

8. Twain lists his source for the details of the cruelty of slavery as Charles Bell, *Fifty Years in Chains or the Life of an American Slave,* New York, 1860. The details of the manacled marching slaves and the girl who is sold on the road are apparently taken (though richly embellished) from Bell's own march to South Carolina (pp. 29–42).

whole of medieval society. "The blunting effects of slavery upon the slaveholder's moral perceptions are known and conceded the world over," he wrote,

> and a privileged class, an aristocracy, is but a band of slaveholders under different name . . . One needs but to hear an aristocrat speak of the classes that are below him to recognize—and in but indifferently modified measure—the very air and tone of the actual slaveholder; and behind these are the slaveholder's spirit, the slaveholder's blunted feeling. They are the result of the same cause in both cases: the possessor's old and inbred custom of regarding himself as a superior being. [*14*, 233–4]

Injustice is inevitable in a society in which one class has a monopoly of privilege and power. It is this vast inequality which brings about the brutal laws whose results the Yankee sees on every hand: the wretches tortured, dying, going mad in Morgan le Fay's dungeon for trivial offenses (*14*, 143–61); the woman dying alone in the smallpox hut for blaspheming the Church (*14*, 280–8); and the young mother hanged for stealing in order to feed her child (*14*, 358–62) —to mention but a few of the more dramatic examples.[9]

9. These episodes and many others are elaborations of incidents that Twain was forever noting in the course of his reading in history. The important task of a thorough scholarly investigation of the sources of the *Yankee* remains to be done but Twain himself lists the following in Notebook 24, pp. 13–15: Lecky, *History of European Morals* and *History of England in the Eighteenth Century;* Charles Bell; J. Hammond Trumbull, *Blue Laws True and False; Encyclopedia Britannica* (for information on interdicts and the Curse of Rome); *Encyclopedia Americana* (for the process of becoming a saint); Carlyle, *French Revolution;* Taine, *Ancient Regime;* Stanley, *Memorials of Westminster Abbey* (for information on the interdict during the reign of King John. Twain is confused here; Stanley says nothing about the interdict but does talk about the thirty-day wearing of chaplets after the Coronation of Henry III. In Notebook 19, p. 29, Twain lists his sources correctly for these two incidents as the *Britannica* and Stanley respectively); Buckle, *History of Civilization in England;*

And always the Church hovers in the background teaching the common people "that patience, humbleness, and the submission to oppression was what He loved to see in parties of subordinate rank" (*14*, 160). Conversely, the cure for injustice lay in spreading political power and social status among the masses by means of universal suffrage: "where every man in the state has a vote, brutal laws are impossible" (*14*, 237).

In the midst of this steady spectacle of human suffering interspersed with occasional optimistic assertions, doubts occasionally creep into the overt statements of the Yankee in his role as spokesman. In one extraordinary passage he denounces training (*14*, 150) and on a later occasion says that he "would like to hang the whole human race and finish the farce"—a clear echo of numerous comments of a similar kind by Twain.[1] This latter remark, to be sure, is closely preceded by the Yankee's observation that "a man is a man, at bottom. Whole ages of abuses and oppression cannot crush the manhood out of him. Whoever thinks it a mistake is himself mistaken. Yes, there is plenty good enough material for a republic in the most degraded people

---

Atlantic Monthly, *24* (1869) (for information on ancient prices—I have been unable to identify with certainty the article to which Twain alludes, though it is perhaps one called "The Old Bankers of Florence," pp. 629–37); an English newspaper of 1885 (for the advertisement reading "Use Peterson's Prophylactic Tooth-Brush—All the Go," carried by a knight [*14*, 167]); Ophelia's burial (apparently for the death of the young girl in the chapter on the smallpox hut [XXIX] and the accompanying "Curse of Rome"); and a cryptic reference to "Rich II" (perhaps an allusion to a passage in Hume's *History of England*. It is listed with Charles Bell as source for the idea that men in slave-holding societies are considered slaves until they prove themselves free). Aside from his general remarks about Catholicism, Twain clearly drew most of the abuses which he attacked in the *Yankee* from the two societies which always fascinated and, at the same time, repelled him the most—the pre-Civil War American South and the *ancien régime*.

1. For the passage on training quoted in full and discussed in detail see below, pp. 139–40.

that ever existed—even the Russians" (*14*, 301). The final result of this juxtaposition of contrary propositions is a kind of stand-off debate, which reflects Twain's own deeply divided mind.

But the official theme of progress is undercut chiefly, not by occasional passages which overtly reveal Twain's doubt, but by what really happens in the book as the result of a conflict stemming from the actions of the principal character. The Yankee changes roles with disconcerting swiftness. After his comments in the passage quoted above, for example, he turns from speculation concerning the political salvation of Russians and Germans to practical matters closer at hand: "We should see certain things yet, let us hope and believe. First a modified monarchy, till Arthur's days were done, then the destruction of the throne, nobility abolished, every member of it bound out to some useful trade, universal suffrage instituted, and the whole government placed in the hands of the men and women of the nation there to remain. Yes, there was no occasion to give up my dream yet awhile" (*14*, 301–2). Obviously the predominantly travel book structure reflects only one of the Yankee's two distinct roles. He is both a passive and an active figure, an observer and a doer. In a travel book, of course, cultural contrasts emerge from the comments of the visitor on his adventures. Normally he does not get involved in the society he examines; certainly he does not change it. The Yankee, on the other hand, not only travels in England, but also builds a complete nineteenth-century civilization there. His Crusoe-like industry imposes, at least potentially, a wholly different structure on the novel—one that is cyclical and shaped by the rise, efflorescence, and final collapse of this artificially induced civilization.

Actually, disregarding scattered references to modern advertising, dynamite bombs, telephones, guns, and newspapers and not counting the final chapters in which some young men with modern weapons emerge from nowhere to help the Yankee, only two chapters (X and XL) out of forty even bother to describe the civilization the Yankee is creating, let alone portray it in action; and in one of the chapters (XL) particularly the description is half-humorous. For reasons we have already discussed (including the technical problems involved in literally superimposing one civilization on another), Twain obviously was not concerned with depicting the Yankee's New Deal in any great detail. Even the nature of his feud with Arnold made him chiefly interested in assaulting the Middle Ages. Ultimately, however, it was his own fundamental skepticism and pessimism which precluded him from dramatizing concretely any kind of easy redemption from human suffering. What is most significant about the role of the Yankee as empire-builder is the fate of the civilization he creates and the relation of this fate to the dreams and psychological drives of the creator.

Read from this point of view, *A Connecticut Yankee* is more than a little similar to that other devastating critique of American optimism, *Moby Dick*. Both Ahab and the Yankee are fabulous, half-symbolic figures—the one with his roots deep in Transcendentalism and Romantic Byronism, the other representative of the questing, enterprising, and, at the same time, aggressive spirit of American industrialism (with *its* roots in Transcendentalism and eighteenth-century rationalism). Both set out to destroy their own particular leviathans, and both are, of course, themselves destroyed in a final cataclysm, Ahab pinioned to his foe, the Yankee trapped by the bodies of those he has slaughtered and prostrate before the leering figure of Merlin. Both, finally, are viewed with a somewhat similar mixture of sympathy and distate by their creators, probably because both figures were, in part at least, projections of unresolved psychic and intellectual problems.[2]

As a character in his own right, the Yankee is a complex figure of diverse origins. In the shadowy background lurks the image of Don Quixote and the despised knightly hero of the "Legend of the Spectacular Ruin" who fights dragons with inductive methods. By 1884 Twain had conceived of a protagonist whose role would be largely burlesque; a well-known notebook entry of that year reads: "Dream of being a knight errant in armor in the Middle Ages. Have the notions and habits of thought of the present day mixed with the necessities of that. No pockets in the armor. Can't scratch . . . Fall down and can't get up." [3] When he sat down to write the opening chapters two years later, however (if we can judge from the chapters themselves, certain notebook entries, and his letter to Mrs. Fairbanks), his attitude toward his entire subject matter was much closer to serious realism, but a realism in which the comic played an important part. At some time during these two years he was forced to choose a hero: someone full of the "notions and habits of the present day" and thus available as spokesman, yet capable of being used, at the same time, in any conceivable comic situation.[4] In his first notes, Twain had imagined the events as happening to himself; but, while he had played such a role occasionally as a young, unknown western writer in *The Innocents Abroad,* he must have felt it impossible for him in 1886. Even in his early work, of course, Twain's tendency was to cast himself in a fairly

2. Richard Chase, without mentioning Twain's Yankee, relates Ahab to nineteenth-century captains of industry and to Yankee folk heroes: *The American Novel and Its Tradition* (New York, 1957), pp. 101–2.

3. Notebook 18 (1884–85), p. 11, published in *Mark Twain's Notebook,* p. 171. For the "Legend of the Spectacular Ruin" see above, pp. 77–8.

4. In Notebook 20 (Aug. 20, 1885 – Jan. 20, 1886), the notes indicate that the hero has been selected. One, for example, reads as follows: "I'll show him that I wasn't brought up on a Connecticut Farm for nothing" (p. 33).

"straight" or respectable role and leave the crude comedy to a vernacular alter ego (e.g. Brown).

Obviously in 1886 some widely representative vernacular figure was needed. Huck, Tom, and Jim were available (indeed, the notebooks of the 1880's are filled with plans for their further adventures), but, in Twain's mind, they were hopelessly associated with the past, with the flush times of the river, with the idyllic village, even with medievalism—never with the industrial present. Besides, Twain needed an adult; in *A Connecticut Yankee* he was going to attempt to work out a solution to the human condition in which the values of childhood would have no part. The *Yankee,* in fact, is a deliberate attempt to repudiate childhood. Arthur and his fellow countrymen are scornfully described as "big children," "modified savages," "great simple-hearted creatures"—naive, full of animal-like loyalty, dirty, slothful, improvident, and deeply irrational (*14,* 21–2, 99, 101, 111). In *A Connecticut Yankee* Twain directs his central assault against what he calls the "loyalty of unreason." The significance of this attack can be measured only if we keep in mind that this kind of loyalty is the stuff from which the relationships of Edward and Miles Hendon and Huck and Jim are made. "It is pure animal," says the Yankee, who proudly describes himself as "the champion of hard unsentimental common sense and reason" (*14,* 386).

In selecting his hero there were other factors which Twain must have taken into consideration. "I wanted to say a Yankee mechanic's say against monarchy and its several natural props," he wrote his English publishers in 1889 (*35,* 524). Twain clearly wanted a *typical* American to answer Arnold and other English critics because only a typical American could really refute in the flesh what Twain believed to be their main contention: namely, that American civilization was radically defective because it lacked culture. The vulgarity, the cultural obtuseness of the Yankee as finally conceived, in other words, is part of the point that Twain was trying to make; he grants the English their argument (as he always did), and then tries to show that vulgarity is better than inhumanity. There is no indication that Twain had any illusions about the limitations of his main character or that these limitations were other than deliberately introduced. "You know," he once told Dan Beard, his illustrator for *A Connecticut Yankee,* "this Yankee of mine has neither the refinement nor the weakness of a college education; he is a perfect ignoramus; he is boss of a machine shop; he can build a locomotive or a Colt's revolver, he can put up and run a telegraph line, but he's an ignoramus, nevertheless" (*33,* 887–8). Twain clearly needed a vernacular hero for far more important reasons than simply to serve as comic butt.

In what was potentially a brilliant choice, he seized upon the figure of the Yankee, one of the archetypal vernacular characters in American humorous writing, the traditional symbol of mocking defiance to English values, yet a figure whose famed ingenuity and practicality made him readily adaptable to the urban industrial culture Twain wished to represent.[5] Twain's elaborately contrived introduction to the main narrative serves both to emphasize the distance between himself and his hero and the particular point of view of the latter. "I am an American," says the stranger who walks into Twain's hotel room.

5. For my general concept of the Yankee type I am indebted to Constance Rourke's magnificent book, *American Humor* (New York, Doubleday, 1953), pp. 15–36. I cannot agree, however, with many of her ideas about Twain, particularly that he always used the Yankee fable innocently and without perspective and that it "grew rigid in his mind." She, for example, takes the Yankee's love of chromos and his opinion of Raphael as necessarily being Twain's own (pp. 172–3) and thus fails to perceive Twain's deliberate and careful vulgarizing of the man. In *The American Claimant,* Mulberry Sellers' walls are covered with what Twain calls "deadly chromos" (*15,* 10–11).

> I was born and reared in Hartford, in the state of Connecticut—anyway, just over the river, in the country. So I am a Yankee of the Yankees—and practical; yes, and nearly barren of sentiment, I suppose—or poetry, in other words. My father was a blacksmith, my uncle was a horse-doctor, and I was both, along at first. Then I went over to the great arms factory and learned my real trade . . . learned to make everything: guns, revolvers, cannon, boilers, engines, all sorts of labor-saving machinery. Why I could make anything in the world . . . and if there wasn't any quick new-fangled way to make a thing, I could invent one —and do it as easy as rolling off a log. I became head superintendent. [*14*, 5]

With his background in rural myth, the Yankee in his own lifetime has made the shift from a country to a city environment—the same shift that so many Americans were making during the nineteenth century. In him the jack-of-all-trades has become transformed into the technician. Matthew Arnold notes in *Civilization in the United States* (p. 92) that Americans were industrious and smart but possessed of a "hard unintelligence," an intellectual mediocrity and vulgarity. The Yankee (probably deliberately) was the very incarnation of his worst fears—the "ignoramus."

Ironically, however, Twain was unconsciously creating at the same time in the portrait of the Yankee and his fate the incarnation of his *own* worst fears. Constance Rourke has pointed out that the traditional Yankee of folklore "was seldom deeply involved in situations." [6] The Boss, on the other hand, is involved in everything; it is this quality of dynamism in his personality which continually threatens to break down the dominant structural

6. *American Humor,* p. 34.

pattern of the book. He is the American speculator of the day, a paler but less sentimentalized Colonel Sellers, a figure whose roots are primarily in the South and West rather than New England.[7] He combines a ruthless desire to dominate any situation in which he finds himself—for instance, his determination, when he first arrives in England, to "boss the whole country inside of three months" (*14,* 16) or his fatal persistence in attacking the Blacksmith (*14,* 322–38)—with the visionary enthusiasm of Colonel Sellers laying out a railroad with his knife and fork. Becoming acclimated to his new environment with amazing rapidity, he can soon think of nothing but "the opportunities here for a man of knowledge, brains, pluck, and enterprise to sail in and grow up with the country. The grandest field that ever was; and all my own; not a competitor; not a man who wasn't a baby to me in acquirements and capacities . . . What a jump I had made! I couldn't keep from thinking about it, and contemplating, just as one does who has struck oil" (*14,* 60–1). Not only can the Yankee be as ruthlessly quick-witted as Simon Suggs, but his humor often has in it a bottom of cruelty such as is found in much western literature. Also clearly western and entirely at variance with his reported practicality is what the Boss calls a "circus" side to his character, his love of grand effects and dramatic climaxes. He is reminiscent of Tom Sawyer in the pleasure he takes planning a slow but colorful escape from the slave-trader. "One could invent quicker ways," he remarks, "and fully as sure ones; but none that would be as picturesque as this;

7. The figure of Colonel Sellers lay in the back of Twain's mind all through the 1880's and undoubtedly influenced the portrait of the Yankee. Some remarks in Notebook 17 (1883–84), p. 26, for example, are apparently ideas for the further adventures of Colonel Sellers—ideas which Howells and Twain at this time were attempting to work into a play. *The American Claimant* (published May, 1892 after previous syndication) was, of course, Twain's first major work after the *Yankee.*

none that could be made so dramatic" (*14*, 356; also 374, 381–2). He is, of course, still building up his effects when he dies.

It is all too easy, nevertheless, to overstress the Americanism of the Yankee and thus, by implication, narrow the themes of the book. He is, above all, representative of industrial man in general; indeed, he is strikingly reminiscent of that other "boss," Napoleon III, whom Twain described admiringly in *The Innocents Abroad* as self-made, shrewd, tough, self-reliant, sympathetic to mechanical and scientific progress and French commercial prosperity and "representative of the highest modern civilization, progress, and refinement." By contrast, Twain saw walking at Napoleon's side in a Paris procession Abdul Aziz, "absolute lord of the Ottoman Empire . . . the repprsentative of a people by nature and training filthy, brutish, ignorant, unprogressive, superstitious—and a government whose Three Graces are Tyranny, Rapacity, Blood. Here in brilliant Paris . . . the First Century greets the nineteenth" (*1*, 119–23). The personal and cultural differences apparent in these two men are essentially the same as those found in the Yankee and King Arthur.

Optimism and pride—and overreaching—are the real keys to the character and fate of Promethean man in all his incarnations. "For such as have brains there are no defeats, but only victories," says the Yankee in what is perhaps his most revealing remark (*14*, 120). It is this faith that is behind his dream of Utopia—behind, in particular, his long struggle with the arch-villainy of the Roman Catholic Church. Almost from the beginning of the book, the Yankee is aware of his real enemy; always, in the background, delaying the arrival of Utopia, ready to overthrow his best work, hover the forces of entrenched superstition symbolized by Twain in the institution of the Church. After four years the Yankee has his nineteenth-century civilization ("fenced away from the public view") booming:

> My schools and churches were children four years before; they were grown up now; my shops of that day were vast factories now; where I had a dozen trained men then, I had a thousand now; where I had one brilliant expert then, I had fifty now. I stood with my hand on the cock, so to speak, ready to turn it on and flood the midnight world with light at any moment. But I was not going to do the thing in that sudden way . . . The people could not have stood it; and, moreover, I should have had the Established Roman Catholic Church on my back in a minute.

A few pages further on the Yankee recounts how he and his "experts" had planned "to survey and map the kingdom, but the priests had always interfered and raised trouble. So we had given the thing up, for the present; it would be poor wisdom to antagonize the churches." Utopia was at hand but human beings apparently were not ready for it; the Yankee can only trust to time and slow change. He decides "to gnaw a little at this and that and the other superstition, and so prepare the way gradually for a better order of things" (*14*, 78–81). At this point in the novel Twain sends the Yankee traveling, and for the next three hundred pages we are presented with the spectacle of every variety of human baseness.

Eventually, however, the Yankee defeats certain hostile English knights in combat, and England is transformed into a "happy and prosperous country"—in Twain's description of which, significantly, the burlesque note is never far beneath the surface. Has human nature really changed for the better and evil been completely rooted out as the Yankee optimistically hopes and plans? Apparently so. The Yankee is riding the crest of power and success.

> I was very happy. Things were working steadily toward a secretly longed-for point. You see, I had two schemes in my head which were the vastest of all my projects. The one was to overthrow the Catholic Church and set up the Protestant faith on its ruins—not as an Established Church, but as a go-as-you-please one; and the other project was to get a decree issued by and by, commanding that upon Arthur's death unlimited suffrage should be introduced. [*14*, 398–400]

The crucial questions thus remain unanswered. The Yankee's ideal state exists only in theory: since he rules as a benevolent dictator, democracy has not been tested in action; and, since he has postponed the struggle with the Church until the ameliorative effects of his own system of training can be felt, the climactic (indeed, the symbolic) contest with evil incarnate is still in the future.

When this final contest is joined, the result, of course, is disaster for the Yankee. He becomes quickly aware that his "dream of a republic is to be a dream and so remain" (*14*, 417). He is quickly disabused of his optimism about human nature when most of his "experts" threaten to desert to the enemy because of their fear of the Interdict. "We haven't sixty faithful left," Clarence informs him bluntly and he replies:

> "What are you saying? Our schools, our colleges, our vast workshops, our—"
>
> "When those knights come, those establishments will empty themselves and go over to the enemy. Did you think you had educated the superstition out of those people?"

> "I certainly did think it."
>
> "Well, then, you may unthink it. They stood every strain easily—until the Interdict. Since then, they merely put on a bold outside—at heart they are quaking. Make up your mind to it—when the armies come, the mask will fall."
>
> "It's hard news. We are lost." [*14*, 42]

Not only do the enlightened fall away, but the slaves fight for their masters; the Yankee experiences at first hand a psychological phenomenon which, as Twain's spokesman on an earlier occasion, he had described as having occurred in the South and as being "depressing" to observe but perhaps not impossible to overcome (*14*, 298–302).

Now his disillusionment is complete and he realizes the folly of his optimism. As the English forces gather against him, he comments bitterly:

> Oh, what a donkey I was! Toward the end of the week I began to get this large and disenchanting fact through my head: that the mass of the Nation had swung their caps and shouted for a republic for about one day, and there an end . . . Why even the very men who had lately been slaves were in the "righteous cause," and glorifying it, praying for it . . . just like all the other commoners. Imagine such human muck as this; conceive of this folly!
>
> . . . Truly this was more than I had bargained for. [*14*, 429–30]

Disgusted with the spectacle of cowardly human nature, the Yankee turns to technology for salvation, but this too betrays him. He himself succumbs to the implacable Merlin, and his few young technician followers die in a monstrous trap of their own making, surrounded by the putrefying dead who lie frozen to the electrified barbed wire or piled up in front of the gatling guns (*14*, 443–6).

The full significance of this incredible scene can only be grasped if we keep in mind that Twain gives a similar fate to the dictator in his later Adamic sketches.[8] In both cases, the "secret weapon" of science ultimately destroys the very people who have sought omnipotence in its hands; it is a harbinger, not of Utopia, but of chaos. Our final picture in chronological terms of the Yankee is of the sick, despairing, and broken old man who wanders through the opening pages of the novel. He has become an outcast from modern times, a man who, in his delirium, finds his reality and his affections rooted in the past and, indeed, considers it a dream that he has been "set down, a stranger and forlorn" in a "strange England" (*14*, 449). In the Yankee's nostalgia for his lost land (further elaborated in a significant notebook entry) Henry Nash Smith finds a reflection of Twain's own nostalgia and his fundamental alienation from the technological society of his maturity.[9] Having bound his protagonist to the wheel of fire, Twain once again made him his spokesman—but for a very different message.

The details of Twain's dénouement to the *Yankee* are almost as important as the general meaning of the whole. His Arthurian materials gave him a ready-made catastrophe. As early as 1886, he had clearly decided to make use of it, for he wrote Mrs. Fairbanks at that time that he "should grieve indeed if the final disruption, and the extinction of . . . old tender and gracious friendships, and that last battle—the Battle of the Broken Hearts, it might be called—should lose their pathos and their tears through

8. See above, p. 40.

9. See "Mark Twain's Images of Hannibal," pp. 27–30. The notebook entry in question says the book will be entitled "The Lost Land" and describes the Yankee's final emotional state in the following way: "He mourns his lost land—has come to England and revisited it, but it is all changed and become old, so old!—and it was so fresh and new, so virgin before" (20, p. 33).

my handling."[10] The notebook reference to the "Lost Land" also dates from around this time. These early comments, nevertheless, suggest only the fact of a catastrophe and the Yankee's final mood; but was he to be the cause of the catastrophe or an innocent victim of internal troubles at Camelot? If anything the letter to Mrs. Fairbanks seems to indicate the latter.

All the notes, however, which date from a time when Twain was well into the book make clear that the central cause of the catastrophe would be the Yankee's conflict with the Church. In Notebook 23(I) for example, Twain wrote the following: "An excommunicated person—carry him through what he had to stand. We assist him—& here begin my troubles & my long fight with the church, & my eventual defeat" (p. 15). On the next page is a description of an interdict which "continues 6 yrs"—an idea which Twain first mentions in 1883 in connection with a little book he was planning to put together someday called "Picturesque Incidents in History."[1] Further on in this same notebook (p. 17) is the comment: "I make a *peaceful* revolution & introduce advanced civilization. The Church overthrows it with a 6 year interdict." Then comes an explanation—and probably Twain's rationalization—of the Yankee's failure: "A revolution cannot be established under 30 years—the men of old ideas must die off." This explanation resembles that of Clarence in the finished novel when he tells the Yankee why only young boys have

10. *Mark Twain to Mrs. Fairbanks,* p. 285.

1. Notebook 19, p. 29. Fred W. Lorch, "Hawaiian Feudalism and Mark Twain's *A Connecticut Yankee in King Arthur's Court," American Literature, 30* (1958), 52, shows that Mark Twain probably got interested in interdicts while doing research for a Hawaiian novel. Apparently his chief source book on earlier Hawaiian customs—Jarves' *History of the Hawaiian Islands*—made much of the comparison between native taboos and Catholic interdicts.

not deserted him (*14*, 442). In the stray notes to the Yankee collected as Paine 91, the idea of excommunication is not mentioned, but the direct conflict between the Church and industrialism receives explicit formulation: "King and Country under an interdict for steam-press etc." In any case, Twain by this time had his central conflict in mind (Arthur's problems seem forgotten) although he was uncertain how he would precipitate the overt contest.

His final solution to this problem significantly deepens the pessimism of the ending. In the published book, the events that culminate in Arthur's death happen off-stage and are narrated by Clarence with almost complete fidelity to the details in Malory except that Launcelot wins the enmity of some of his fellow knights, not by rescuing Guinevere from Maliagrance, but by fleecing them through stock manipulation. The resulting civil war serves as the pretext for the interdict which destroys the Yankee's society and leads to open war. The *ultimate* cause of the war, Twain stresses here as in his notebooks, is the inevitability of a showdown between progressivism and the forces of evil. When the Yankee asks Clarence how the crisis came about, for example, the boy answers: "Well, if there hadn't been any Queen Guenever, it wouldn't have come so early; but it would have come, anyway. It would have come on your own account by and by" (*14*, 413). In the book, nevertheless, the precipitating agent that brings on disaster, war, ruin is clearly a vice of the Yankee's own society—namely, stock-market speculation (*14*, 414). The fact that Twain treats the speculation almost as another joke (the Yankee mourns that in the conflict one of the best players on the knights' baseball team was killed) does not change its essential significance to the book. Actually, the tone of all the later chapters runs the gamut from bad humor to maudlin sentimentality, but this only suggests the extent of Twain's mixed emotions regarding the Yankee and his unwillingness at this time in his life to confront directly the full implications of what he was describing.

The extent of these mixed emotions can be verified independently on the strength of other evidence. In 1886, while engaged in a lawsuit against John Wanamaker for selling Grant's *Memoirs* below the publisher's price, Twain called Wanamaker a "close-fisted Connecticut Yankee."[2] He hated Wanamaker and elsewhere described him as an "odorous pilgrim" (because he taught Sunday School) and as "the only individual in a population of 60,000,000 who is known to have picked the pockets of the dead General Grant."[3] Associations such as these must have played their subtle role in shaping the fate of the Yankee and all that he represents.

The final pages of *A Connecticut Yankee* clearly reveal Twain's essential skepticism about history as a faith at a time when he was apparently most optimistic about the future of America and Europe. If the official theme of the book is the progress that Western Society has made since the Middle Ages, the theme of the Yankee's own story, on the contrary, is the absurdity of optimism and the impermanence of progress (or the illusory nature of progress) because of the aggressiveness and rapacity of modern industrial man, the false promise of technology and—ultimately—because of the deep-rootedness of human evil. A recent critic has pointed out that Twain's projected Hawaiian novel was to end with the triumph of old superstitions over the Christianized hero.[4] "There are in Connecticut, at this moment and in all countries," Twain wrote in 1888, "children and disagreeable relatives chained in cellars, all

2. This epithet is attached to Wanamaker in Notebook 21, p. 32. For the details of the lawsuit see *Mark Twain, Business Man,* ed. S. C. Webster (Boston, 1946), pp. 361–5.

3. *Mark Twain in Eruption,* pp. 348–9.

4. Lorch, "Hawaiian Feudalism," pp. 56–7.

sores . . . and vermin . . . This is to suggest that the thing in man which makes him cruel to a slave is in him permanently and will not be rooted out for a million years."[5] Along with this undercurrent of pessimism about human nature, his notebooks during the 80's for the first time contain ideas for fantasies concerning the future of America, one of which was to bear important fruit in later years: "For a play: America in 1985. The Pope here & an Inquisition. The age of darkness back again. Pope is temperal despot, *too.* A titled [canceled: "eccles"] aristocracy & primogeniture. [canceled: "No"] Europe is *republican* & full of science and invention—none allowed here."[6] Significantly, on the page before this note Twain talks about a "wall street play" dealing with the making and losing of fortunes and stock manipulation. Both of these notes, moreover, occur in the same folder that contains projected plans for Colonel Sellers. It is from such doubts and fears as these that Twain created the end of *A Connecticut Yankee.* The Yankee's invasion of England sets in motion an entire cycle of history—from darkness to darkness. In a book on the past, Twain thus makes a major statement, not only about the America of his own day, but (perhaps half-unwittingly) about its future prospects.

The götterdämmerung in the final chapters of the *Yankee* marks the end of an era in which Twain's theory of history was sharply at variance with his intuitions and his deepest convictions. From 1890 on, under the impact of personal tragedy, he was gradually to reshape his theories and bring them more into accordance with his mature vision. The first step in this direction was taken in 1892 with the publication of *The American Claimant.* Written for money after the failure of the Paige typesetter and the

5. Notebook 23(I), p. 16, published in *Notebook,* p. 199.
6. Notebook 17 (1883–84), p. 32.

break-up of his Hartford home and at least partly (according to Paine) at the instigation of those who wanted him to do a novel on the theories of George or Bellamy, the book is a weird mixture of injected social commentary and warmed-over Beriah Sellers. But in it, significantly, the United States is no longer simply the yardstick of social progress but also the society measured—this time by an English aristocrat who believes idealistically in the equality of all men. "I wish to retire from what to me is a false existence," the young Viscount Berkeley tells his sneering father, ". . . and begin my life over again . . . on the level of mere manhood, unassisted by factitious aids, and succeed or fail by pure merit or the want of it. I will go to America, where all men are equal and all have an equal chance" (*15*, 6).

His brave remarks are accompanied on Twain's part by a good many of the usual satiric thrusts at aristocratic institutions and sham romanticism. The point of view in the early chapters of the *Claimant* is scarcely different in substance from *The Innocents Abroad;* and, indeed, Twain's initial description of the ambivalent Sally Sellers is a final summation of the sharp dichotomy between America and Europe developed in his first book. As the daughter of the American claimant, she appropriately went to "Rowena-Ivanhoe College . . . the selectest and most aristocratic seat of learning for young ladies in our country" (*15*, 37). On the other hand, because her father was poverty-stricken, she gladly and capably helped earn the family bread with her own hands. Sally was thus both European and American—both "practical and democratic" and "romantic and aristocratic." "All day she was American, practically, and proud of the work of her head and hands and its commercial result; all the evening she took holiday and dwelt in a rich shadowland peopled with titled and coroneted fictions" (*15*, 49–50). In this portrait of Sally, as in his tedious caricature of the Earl of Rossmore in the opening chapter, Twain was obviously attempting to breathe life into a point of view that had served him well in the past. But satire, as James Sutherland has noted, is the art of persuasion; it rests on powerful convictions and a compulsion to force people to act on these convictions.[7] Where the satire in *The Innocents Abroad* is fresh, spontaneous, often joyful because animated by a coherent historical vision, in the *Claimant* it is forced and mechanical (and quickly dropped) because this same vision is largely absent. Behind the façade of music-hall comedy and romance in the latter book a message of defeat and despair was beginning to take shape.

When the Viscount Berkeley arrives in America, he lives for a time in a cheap boarding house and associates with radical groups. One of these groups gives a lecture in which Matthew Arnold is attacked by name and American irreverence and material progress (largely the creation of "humble, unlettered, un-college-bred inventors") defended (*15*, 79–85). But the Viscount's subsequent adventures in America serve only to prove the falsity of the lecturer's thesis; rebuffed on all sides in his search for a job because of lack of money and influence, the disillusioned Englishman finally returns to England to reassume the titles he had renounced. He has learned by this time that "in a republic where all are free and equal prosperity and position constitute rank" and "misfortune is a crime" (*15*, 108–10). Significantly, the lecture that the Viscount hears as an ingenuous equalitarian is actually Twain's transcription of at least one of his own unpublished articles written at the height of his quarrel with Arnold.[8] In other words, Twain uses the angry and passionate convictions of his earlier years for ironic purposes in *The American Claimant*.

7. *English Satire* (Cambridge, 1958), pp. 4–5.
8. See Paine 102a.

The truth—if we are to assign any weight to the Viscount's experience—is something very different again.

The idea that prosperity and position constituted rank in America did not, of course, first dawn on Twain in 1892. In *The Innocents Abroad,* for instance, an Italian who has visited America remarks to his fellows that money buys honor and power there. The qualities of American life that the Italian stresses, however, are those familiar democratic values that we have already noted as making up Twain's image of the nineteenth century: irreverence, freedom, education, and material prosperity for all. Twain (whatever his hidden doubts) was still stressing these values in 1889 and apologizing for American materialism in terms of historical perspective. "We Americans worship the almighty dollar," he noted around this time and then added: "Well, it is a worthier God than Hereditary Privilege." [9] But by 1892 in *The American Claimant* it is fairly clear that one sort of worship is as morally destructive as another, that it is, moreover, futile to struggle by personal example against inequality because of the inertia of human nature. The Viscount learns that the faults of any aristocracy lie not with the aristocrats themselves but "with the mass of people who allow it to exist and who long to enter it themselves" (*15,* 129–31). Defeated though now worldly-wise, he admits his own aristocratic instincts and the futility of trying to change the attitudes of others by personal example. In the end, he is willing, as he writes his father, to leave "further experiment of a missionary sort to other young people needing the chastening and quelling persuasions of experience, the only logic sure to convince a diseased imagination and restore it to rugged health" (*15,* 214).

That Mulberry Sellers remains the strongest exponent of science and optimism in *The American Claimant* only

9. Notebook 24, pp. 26–7, published in *Notebook,* p. 209.

suggests further the utter disintegration of the image of progress in Twain's mind. He is an impotent Yankee, a man without force or power who ceaselessly dreams of miraculous technological discoveries (one of which, incidentally, will "materialize" good people who have died and restock the corrupt governments of the world with them). Among Sellers' grandiose plans is one to establish a Russian republic, and he comments breathlessly to his friend Washington Hawkins that "we live in wonderful times. The elements are crowded *full* of beneficent forces—always *have* been—and ours is the first generation to turn them to account and make them work for us. Why, Hawkins, *everything* is useful—*nothing* ought ever to be wasted. Now look at sewer-gas for instance" (*15*, 159–60). It is as if in the figure of Sellers Twain set out deliberately to caricature the Yankee in the same fashion that elsewhere in the book he undercut his earlier essays on Arnold. To the cold and complacent acceptance of human nature suggested by the actions of the Viscount all that Twain could counterpoise in 1892 was the fatuous and empty rhetoric of the American salesman. Sellers was, in Twain's sardonic words, "always keeping breast to breast with the drum major in the great work of material civilization" (*15*, 62).

What in *A Connecticut Yankee* must be largely implied from the fate of the hero is thus, in the *Claimant*, becoming more and more overt. The institutions of democracy, apparently, could not change man's nature permanently or possibly even at all through "training." From such a supposition, Twain was later to conclude that the progress of civilization was at best highly transitory and at worst nonexistent. *The American Claimant* marked the beginning of a conscious and radical reformulation of his interpretation of history. A decade later the issue would be clear enough. In the margin of a writer who was arguing that we must work to preserve the gains of the French and American Revolutions from "the foxes and wolves of politics and superstition" Twain wrote emphatically: "But then the modern human race is frankly devoted to the game of grab, just as the race was earlier devoted to piety & hypocrisy." [1]

1. S. V. M. D. Clevenger, *The Evolution of Man and His Mind* (Chicago, 1903), p. 49; MTP.

Part Three

ESCAPE FROM HISTORY

7.

STRATEGIES OF ESCAPE: HUCK AND HISTORY

Full of doubt I stand
Whether I should repent me now of sin
By me done or occasioned, or rejoice
Much more that much more good thereof
Shall spring—
Paradise Lost, XII, 473–6

Chronological organization, we must remind ourselves, has only a limited relevance when we are describing the work of Mark Twain. The book which deals most emphatically with piety, hypocrisy, and the "game of grab" was begun in 1876 and published in 1884. In Twain's greatest novel some of his deepest and most enduring feelings and convictions were at last to find an "answerable style." This chapter is not a comprehensive organic criticism of *Huckleberry Finn.* Indeed, it leans heavily on the exhaustive and often brilliant exegesis to which the book has been subjected in recent years. Rather it attempts to explore in some detail the intellectual and imaginative nexus that finds complete and coherent expression in *Huckleberry Finn;* it traces the elements which, in their momentary coalescence, formed a masterpiece.

In *Life on the Mississippi,* as we have already observed, two very different themes are developed at some length:

on the one hand, the progress of society on the banks of the river from feudalism to democracy and industrialism; on the other, the values of life on the river itself—freedom, independence, essential innocence, escape from society, and, ultimately, escape from the tyranny of time and history. The first of these themes is, of course, dominant in *Life on the Mississippi;* sometimes reluctantly, sometimes exuberantly, Twain embraced the historical process. The development of human institutions from barbarism to civilization would mitigate, if not solve, the problem of human evil. Where proper influences were brought to bear on mankind, it would no longer be necessary to worry about the human condition. "Solicitude for the future of a race like this is not in order," he advised the reader regarding the population of the Northwest.

But as his treatment of the Yankee surely attests, Twain could not follow his own advice. In a curious fashion, during the very years in which he became a vociferous celebrant of historical progress, his pessimism, always latent, was steadily deepening and more and more finding expression. The extremes of the 80's suggest heroic attempts at compensation. It was as if his reading about the cruelties of the past, his recovery of childhood memories, his own mature experience, and his sense of guilt made some kind of hope and faith even more necessary for him. Perhaps evil could be exorcised by labeling it with a date and location. Doubts, however, continually broke through the fragile surface of Twain's historical optimism. In a letter to Howells (1884) regarding the scandal and vituperation of the Blaine-Cleveland campaign, for example, he sounded a note of a deeper import than the principles of his growing political liberalism. "Isn't human nature the most consummate sham and lie that was ever invented?" he wrote. "Isn't man a creature to be ashamed of in pretty much all of his aspects? Man, 'know thyself'—and then thou wilt despise thyself, to a dead moral certainty" (*35*, 443). We are reminded of how Huck was "ashamed of the human race" as he observed the cold-blooded hypocrisy of the king and the duke sobbing over the death of Wilks (hypocrisy matched only by the sentimentality and gullibility of the townspeople). This episode, like so many others in the book, goes beyond mere satire on aristocratic institutions to become a fundamental comment on the baseness of human nature.

Certainly if his notebooks are any indication, Twain's return to the Mississippi Valley suggested to him immediate conclusions about human nature and human destiny far less sanguine than his later advice to his readers not to worry about the future of the human race. "The histories of Will Bowen, Sam & Capt. McClure and Mrs. B. make human life appear a grisly & hideous sarcasm," he comments at one point. Later in the same notebook comes the following: "Human nature cannot be studied in cities except at a disadvantage—a village is the place. There you can know your man inside and out—in a city you but know his crust; & his crust is usually a lie." Behind the veil of decent or indecent hypocrisy loomed the horror of reality. Where human beings were not willfully cruel, they were stupidly cruel. Among these same notes is recorded the story of the deaf child whose mother unwittingly boxed its ears for what seemed like inattentiveness.[1] When this story appeared later in *Huckleberry Finn*, it was, significantly, the good and kindly Jim who was made the parent. In other words, the very measure of the Negro's humanity is his fallibility. In the face of such radical human imperfection, of how much help were libraries, public education,

1. Notebook 16 (1882), pp. 27, 49, 53. The note on the boxed ears was published in Bernard De Voto, *Mark Twain at Work* (Cambridge, Mass., Harvard Univ. Press, 1942), p. 69. For the incident as used in the completed book see *Works, 13*, 215–16.

scientific marvels, and free institutions? Twain seemed to answer this question in another note of the same time: "Who can think wise or stupid things at all that were not thought of in the past." [2] A year later he sketched in his notebook the outline of a play in which America would return to an "age of darkness" around 1985.[3] By the early 80's and probably before, Twain was thus quietly forging the materials out of which he would shape late in life his explicit denial of historical progress.

Twain's belief in progress, in short, provided a tenuous and shaky counterbalance to the growing weight of his pessimism. What seemed to be an infallible theory was everywhere perverted to darker ends by the empirical evidence and inner agony. The theory itself was deceptively simple: man is shaped solely by heredity and institutions; his heredity is a constant and his institutions are getting better; therefore, man must be getting better. Even in as late an essay as "What Is Man?" (1896, printed 1906), the philosophical underpinnings of Twain's theory of progress remain secure. Here he argues (as he had in 1883 before the Monday Evening Club) that man's only innate impulse is self-interest but that this impulse can be shaped and developed by outside influences, indeed, only by these influences. Our training determines our sense of duty. "Training is potent. Training toward higher and higher . . . ideals is worth any man's thought and labor and diligence." Man is a chameleon; "by the law of his nature he takes the color of his place of resort." Since all impulses toward social development must be externally initiated, outside influences or accidents start us on the road to change. Twain explicitly denies the "intuitive perception of good and evil," but this is unnecessary for progress; training can lead us to perfection—at least

2. Notebook 16, p. 54.
3. See above, p. 127.

up to the limits of our temperament (i.e. our heredity factor).[4] Evil must be, therefore, largely the result of faulty institutions. After Morgan le Fay, for example, has casually knifed a page who brushed against her knee, the Yankee glibly explains that "she was a result of generations of training in the unexamined and unassailed belief that the law which permitted her to kill a subject when she chose was a perfectly right and righteous one" (*14*, 151). The villain of the piece, in other words, was not Morgan le Fay but the Dark Ages.

But the Yankee (or rather Twain speaking through the Yankee) does not rest on this conclusion. Shortly before he, in effect, excuses Morgan le Fay, he has burst into a passionate confession, probably the most extraordinary passage in a book where anomalies abound:

> Training—training is everything; training is all there is *to* a person. We speak of nature; it is folly; there is no such thing as nature; what we call by that misleading name is merely heredity and training. We have no thoughts of our own, no opinions of our own; they are transmitted to us, trained into us. All that is original in us, and therefore fairly creditable or discreditable to us can be covered up and hidden by the point of a cambric needle, all the rest being atoms contributed by, and inherited from, a procession of ancestors that stretches back a billion years to the Adam-clam or grasshopper or monkey from whom our race has been so tediously and ostentatiously and unprofitably developed. And as for me, all that I think about in this plodding sad pilgrimage, this pathetic drift between the eternities, is to look out and humbly live

4. *Works, 26,* 1–61. Alexander E. Jones, "Mark Twain and the Determinism of *What Is Man?*" *American Literature, 29* (1957), 1–17, also points out that Twain's determinism could theoretically serve as a doctrine of hope as well as despair.

> a pure and high and blameless life, and save that one microscopic atom in me that is truly *me:* the rest may land in sheol and welcome for all I care. [*14,* 150]

That such an idea should be put in the mind of one who is presumably dedicated to developing the factory system in order "to turn groping and grubbing automata into *men*" (*14,* 147) is nothing short of incredible. Twain's determinism is a two-edged sword and here it completely cuts the ground from under the official theme of his novel. Denied is any meaning, historical or otherwise, to human experience (life is a "pathetic drift between eternities"); denied is the virtue of training—*any* kind of training—which has served to separate us from our human and animal ancestors (from whom we have been so "unprofitably developed"); and denied, of course, is the value of any traits that may have been inherited. The only positive value in life is "that one microscopic atom in me that is truly *me*"—in other words, something, anything in man that is not subject to time and history, something, indeed, that time and history destroy. Theoretically man could achieve salvation only in society; actually, society was both symbol and cause of his damnation. All that was left for men was denunciation ("the rest may land in sheol and welcome") and flight. All euphemisms aside, Mark Twain's fundamental attitude was "to hell with civilization." In this one paragraph at least, *A Connecticut Yankee* pointed directly backward to *Huckleberry Finn* and forward to "Hadleyburg" and *The Mysterious Stranger.* Clearly, even during the period of Twain's most complete intellectual commitment to progress, one side of his nature was using the very theories on which this commitment was based as a weapon against it and casting about for substitute values.

The relationship merely hinted at in the Yankee's speech between values apart from history and history itself can be seen more precisely if we first of all examine the whole problem in its later manifestations. With the final abandonment near the end of his life of what had previously been a major premise (i.e. that certain institutions "trained" men to better ends than others) Twain's rigid determinism became completely subservient to his historical pessimism. If every institution had its own peculiar set of evils, all training was in some way corrupting; man was, indeed, born selfish and then made worse. He was, as Twain enjoyed pointing out, worse than an animal because an animal had only its natural inheritance to worry about: "*Inborn nature* is character, by itself, in the brutes . . . inborn nature *and* the modifying conscience ["the creature of training"], working together, make character in man." [5] With an animal there was no danger that natural evils would be compounded by the sins of society, but only man before the Fall (i.e. before he entered history) was in a similarly enviable state—perhaps, indeed, more enviable since man before the Fall was free even from the taint of heredity. It is essentially for this reason that Twain, during much of his life but especially in his later years, was so fascinated by Adam and Eve.

The significance of Adam and Eve for Twain (aside from the fact that they were handy vehicles for his sentimental and burlesque propensities) is most clearly evident in those fugitive sketches which Bernard de Voto collected under the titles of "Letters from the Earth" and "Papers of the Adam Family." In these sketches and others that he never got around to writing, Twain apparently planned to describe the course of American and, by extension, all human history in terms of the biblical story of man from the Creation to the Flood. In its completed form, Twain's narrative of the Adam family would have described life in the Garden of Eden, the Fall, a period of Jeffersonian

5. Notebook 32(I), p. 2, published in *Notebook*, p. 349. Italics are Twain's.

democracy, then a period of wealth and high civilization under the aegis of industrialism, and, finally, a spiritual collapse followed by a "dark age" of political and religious dictatorship.

All history was, of course, the result of the initial Fall, at which time man became vulnerable to the knowledge of evil or, in Twain's phraseology, acquired the "moral sense." Rightly understood, Twain's denunciation of the moral sense was an attack on the process of history; for Adam's Fall, as he conceived it, resulted less in making man forevermore innately sinful (i.e. *born with* an original sin) than in making him *after birth* vulnerable to training in sin because of his conscience. To put it in Freudian terms, the burden of the Fall was not the id but the super-ego. In no way could the Fall be considered "fortunate" because Twain denied the redemptive agency of the conscience. Rather, it was a mysterious instrument which rendered man helpless in the presence of corrupting institutions. Not that his comments are without ambivalence in the Adamic sketches; here, as elsewhere, they have their strong Promethean side. His God is cruel, vengeful, and jealous of his position. "Man is so made," wrote Twain, "that he eagerly wants to know: whereas the priest like God, whose imitator and representative he is, has made it his business from the beginning to help him from knowing any useful thing." In Eden, moreover, he makes Adam a budding scientist.[6] But his heavy stress on the curse of conscience reflects, in part, the personal guilt he felt all his life, later augmented by the tragedies of the 90's.

"My conscience is a part of *me*," Twain wrote in his notebook in the late 90's. "It is a mere [canceled: "function"] machine, like my heart—but moral, not physical; and being moral, is teachable [canceled: "and"] its actions

6. "Letters from the Earth," pp. 22, 39.

modifiable. It is merely a *thing;* the creature of training; it is whatever one's mother & Bible & comrades and laws & system of government & habitat & heredities have made it. It is not a separate person, it has no originality, no independence." [7] The whole idea of modesty, for example, illustrated for Twain how the moral sense corrupts. "Adam and Eve entered the world naked and unashamed—naked and pure-minded," he noted in one of his "Letters from the Earth"; "and no descendant of theirs has ever entered it otherwise. All have entered it naked, unashamed, and clean in mind. They have entered it modest. They had to acquire immodesty and the soiled mind, there was no other way to get it." And he added: "The convention miscalled modesty has no standard and cannot have one because it is opposed to nature and reason, and is therefore an artificiality and subject to anybody's whim, anybody's diseased caprice." [8] Here Twain apparently conceives of man as being born innocent and corrupted by training of any kind. At other times we have observed that he stressed the burden of man's inherited temperament. But heredity, however much it rendered absurd the hope of human freedom, offered at least the possibility of goodness. Training destroyed both freedom and any chance of goodness. Every man's life, in short, reduplicated the Fall of Adam to the extent that he became contaminated by society. This idea is implicit in Twain's letter to Howells explaining why he had not taken Tom Sawyer beyond boyhood: "If I went on now, and took him into manhood, he would just lie, like all the one-horse men in literature, and the reader

7. Notebook 32(I), p. 2.

8. Cf. his remarks to Elinor Glynn in 1908 (*Mark Twain in Eruption,* pp. 315–16). Here Twain defends convention against the laws of nature and God "which would soon plunge us into confusion and disorder and anarchy, if we should adopt them." These two passages juxtaposed suggest clearly how Twain vacillated between his dream of individual freedom and his faith (however qualified) in human institutions.

would conceive a hearty contempt for him" (*34*, 258).

If innocence and innate goodness were to be found at all, therefore, they would be found in the heart of a very young and very ignorant child. Adam and Eve, his archetypal innocents, Twain describes as being "children, and ignorant."[9] They cannot do wrong because they have no notion of the concept (the moral sense teaches only wrong). As Satan tells Eve in the Garden: "Whatever you and they [animals] do is right and innocent. It is a divine estate, the loftiest and purest attainable in heaven and on earth. It is the angel gift" (*29*, 343). After eating the apple, Eve gets old and symbolically enters history; she becomes the prototype of all the boys and girls who grow up to lie and suffer and betray themselves. Again and again in his descriptions of children, Twain echoes the dream of Eden that he has put in the mouth of Satan. The sisters of Tom Canty (and, by extension, Tom himself) in *The Prince and the Pauper,* for example, are "good-hearted girls, unclean, clothed in rags, and profoundly ignorant" (*11*, 4). Likewise the children of Domremy were "just of the ordinary peasant type; not bright, of course . . . but good-hearted and companionable, obedient to their parents and the priests; and as they grew up they became properly stocked with narrownesses and prejudices got at second-hand from their elders, and adopted without reserve; and without examination also—which goes without saying. Their religion was inherited, their politics the same" (*17*, 6). Here both Eden and the Fall are described as they work out in the life of a society. For Twain, the essential miracle of Joan of Arc herself is that she could carry into later life the goodness and innocence of her youth in the teeth of her feudal en-

9. "Love, peace, comfort, measureless contentment—that was life in the Garden. It was a joy to be alive. Interests were abundant; for we were children, and ignorant" ("Letters from the Earth," p. 106). In another place, Eve reminisces of "that old simple, ignorant time" when she and Adam did not know they were founding the human race (p. 124).

vironment. She is accordingly, a Christ figure, an incarnation of the "divine estate" which Satan praises in Eve.

All miracles aside, however, it is the rebel and outcast Huck Finn who is Twain's most complete and vivid embodiment of instinctive goodness. Twain made his most explicit statement of the meaning of Huck's personality and experiences in a series of notes for a lecture to be delivered during his tour of Washington and Northwest Canada in 1895. "I should exploit the proposition [in my lecture] that in a crucial moral emergency a sound heart is a safer guide than an ill-trained conscience. I sh'd support this doctrine with a chapter from a book of mine where a sound heart & a deformed conscience come into collision & conscience suffers defeat," he wrote in his notebook. Then follows a sketch of the story: two bosom friends (Huck and Jim) are brought together by misfortune; Huck is a child of neglect, shunned by the respectable community; he has his father's conscience and that of the other townspeople regarding Negroes. "It shows," said Twain, pointing the moral of this situation, "that that strange thing, the conscience—that unerring monitor—can be trained to approve [canceled: "& uphold"] any wild thing you want it to approve if you begin its education early and stick to it." [1] Huck's struggle with his conscience has often been described as a brilliant technical device for the achievement of irony. But it is more than a device: it is nothing less than a direct reflection of Twain's deepest convictions. And the irony cuts deep, not only into the pretensions of that Jeffersonian village society on which Twain himself would look back with such longing at various times in his life, but also, more importantly, into all the false hopes of history. After the Fall there was no New Jerusalem which the descendants of Adam could hope to reach, wiser and more mature through their experience in history. What

1. Notebook 28a(1) [1895], p. 36.

had been lost was worth more than anything that could be gained. All an adult could do (in the Yankee's words) was "to look out and humbly live a pure and high and blameless life, and save that one microscopic atom in one that is truly *me*." From this point of view life in society was, at best, simply a long delaying action against corruption.

Before turning to a more extensive examination of *Huckleberry Finn,* we must look briefly at *The Prince and the Pauper,* an early result of the same intellectual ferment that produced *Life on the Mississippi, Huckleberry Finn,* and eventually *A Connecticut Yankee.* It is a book which closely reflects the themes, imagery, and much of the subject matter of these three other artistically greater works. In *The Prince and the Pauper* are the same attacks on feudalism and false romance, the same hatred of mobs and small town provincialism, the same generally pessimistic picture of human nature, and the same appeal to the natural goodness of children. Tom Canty and his counterpart Prince Edward are amalgamations of the characters of Tom Sawyer and Huckleberry Finn; their vision is clouded and distorted by false romanticism as the story begins, but they learn from their suffering to see life clearly and honestly for what it is—to see (using Twain's metaphor in *Life on the Mississippi*) the snags beneath the picturesque surface of the river. Tom Canty comes from essentially the same poor and depraved background as Huck; both have cruel and drunken fathers who are killed or disappear; both (this time with Prince Edward as Tom) make friends and take up with fellow outcasts and victims of injustice; and both take representative tours through society.[2] Altogether *The*

2. Walter Blair, "When Was *Huckleberry Finn* Written?" *American Literature, 30* (1958), pp. 1–25, argues persuasively that Twain wrote a significant part of *Huckleberry Finn* before he returned to the river in 1882, that much of the book was written more or less simultaneously with *The Prince and the Pauper.* This surely is a major reason for the persistent

Prince and the Pauper is a significant enough book to warrant our taking a closer look at it than it has hitherto received.

In its official theme *The Prince and the Pauper* bears close resemblance to *A Connecticut Yankee.* "My idea," Twain wrote Howells during the later stages of its composition, "is to afford a realizing sense of the exceeding severity of the laws of that day by inflicting some of their penalties upon the King himself and allowing him a chance to see the rest of them applied to others—all of which is to account for certain mildnesses which distinguished Edward VI's reign from those that preceded and followed it" (*34,* 377). Just as in the *Yankee,* Twain's treatment of these laws in *The Prince and the Pauper* is frankly anachronistic; both books are compendiums of the worst features of English and European social legislation from the sixth to the nineteenth century (though the latter makes more of a passing bow to verisimilitude).[3]

In his original preface to the *Yankee,* Twain specifically discusses the Connecticut Blue Laws and points out that they were milder than English legislation of the same period: "There was never a time when America applied the death-penalty to more than fourteen crimes. But England, within the memory of men still living, had in her list of crimes 223 which were punishable by death" (*33,* 1656). This passage closely parallels a paragraph in his "General Note" at the end of *The Prince and the Pauper:* "There has never been a time—under the Blue-Laws or any other —when above FOURTEEN crimes were punishable by death in Connecticut. But in England, within the memory of men who are still hale in body and mind, TWO HUNDRED AND

parallelism between the two. Blair's article is incorporated in his recent *Mark Twain and Huck Finn,* Berkeley, 1960.

3. For Twain's elaborate attempt to work up the social background of this book see Leon T. Dickinson, "The Sources of *The Prince and the Pauper,*" *Modern Language Notes, 14* (1949), 103–6.

TWENTY-THREE crimes were punishable by death!" (*11*, 281). The similarity here is so striking as to suggest not only the identical impulse behind the two books but also that Twain, in writing the Yankee, must have re-examined *The Prince and the Pauper* and the historical materials used in this book. In his own list of the sources of *A Connecticut Yankee* Twain lists Trumbull's *Blue Laws, True and False*.[4] Perhaps another result of this re-examination is the use of almost identical plot devices for revealing the enormity of social injustice: in both books, the kings inadvertently become wandering outcasts and are forced to "go to school to their own laws" in order to "learn mercy" (*11*, 224)—the words are Edward's and express his revelation and his hope.

Edward and Arthur are noble and courageous individuals, who tower above the craven and persecuting mobs which are always nipping at their heels. But only Edward "learns mercy," and he "learns" it only because he can still instinctively respond to human suffering. Arthur, great as he is in his own way (as the Yankee comes to recognize), can only respond to the demands of his own code. When he remains in the smallpox hut, for example, he does so, Twain stresses, primarily because he "considered his knightly honor at stake" (*14*, 282). Not that Arthur is without feelings of pity in this scene; the point is simply that his first and primary response is always (to use Twain's dichotomy) to his "moral sense" rather than his "heart." On another occasion he tells the Yankee that "his conscience . . . was troubling him" because he had encountered two young men escaping from their cruel lord and was doing nothing to catch them and turn them in. Subsequently, he urges on the mob after these men and refuses to cut down a hanged (but apparently still living) man from a tree because, as he puts it, "if he hanged himself, he was

4. See above, p. 110, n. 9.

willing to lose his property to his lord; so let him be. If others hanged him, belike they had the right—let him hang" (*14*, 291–4).

These are responses which move within the narrow limitations of what Twain considered to be a medieval and aristocratic code of conduct, and their contrast with those of both Edward and Huck Finn in similar situations is obvious and startling. *Adult* kings apparently can not "learn mercy" by going "to school to their own laws." The Yankee castigates Arthur in terms more concrete but, nevertheless, similar in tone to those he had used earlier on the vicious Morgan le Fay: "He could see only one side of it [i.e. the debate on whether or not to try to catch the escaped peasants]. He was born so, educated so, his veins were full of ancestral blood that was rotten with this sort of unconscious brutality, brought down by inheritance from a long procession of hearts that had each done its share toward poisoning the stream." The escape of these men, subject, as they were, to the will and pleasure of their lord, was an insult and outrage, "a thing not to be countenanced by any conscientious person who knew his duty to his sacred caste" (*14*, 291–2). On the king, in other words, lay the full burden of the Fall. Beyond any hope of redemption he was cursed with the moral sense—that curious concept which in Twain's hands really becomes an attempt (evident enough in the above passage) to describe the influence, not only of one's immediate environment, but of what Faulkner has aptly called the "entailed birthright" of the past.[5] Clearly Arthur could not himself ameliorate a society which, even before he was born, had already claimed him as its most important victim. Only a deus ex machina, an external force which presumably represented "better" environmental training, could effect changes. Significantly, however, the Yankee's changes are burlesqued,

5. *Absalom, Absalom!* (New York, Random House, 1951), p. 361.

shunted into the background, and finally wiped out, while Twain keeps a steady focus on the spectacle of human suffering and human inertia caused by the moral sense. In *A Connecticut Yankee* Twain put his entire faith in progress and that faith wavered badly. "There are times," admits the Yankee at one point, "when one would like to hang the whole human race and finish the farce" (*14*, 303).

In *The Prince and the Pauper,* on the other hand, Twain combined his official theme of Whig progressivism with the dream of innate goodness which, during this time, was so integral a part of his image of childhood. The book contains the same kind of duality of values that I have already noted in *Life on the Mississippi,* but in *The Prince and the Pauper* there is less sense of potential disparity because the antisocial values are used for social ends. In a fairy story (and only there) Tom Canty masquerading as an absolute monarch could achieve the kind of omnipotence that allowed him magically to set things right in society before society destroyed the goodness he was born with. The reign of Edward VI was, of course, an ideal vehicle for Twain's purposes. Not only had the Somerset protectorate, with its firm Protestantism and its retreat from the pure absolutism of Henry VIII, received the seal of approval of the Whig historians, but also, and more important, the alleged personal qualities of the boy king were those to which Twain was sure to respond. "How his name shines out of the midst of that long darkness," he once wrote, at the same time arguing that Edward was the only good English ruler before Victoria.[6] The tone of this comment is close to that which Twain used normally when talking about Joan of Arc and suggests how much Joan was simply a feminized and somewhat more grown-up Edward.

6. "Notes to Discarded Portions of the *Connecticut Yankee,*" Paine 91a, p. 6. The position of this note suggests again the close link between the *Yankee* and *The Prince and the Pauper.*

Both (in contrast to Arthur) were miraculous exceptions to all the laws of history as Twain conceived them, yet individuals who had somehow made an impact on history—individuals who at least had managed to illuminate the darkness briefly with their own innocence. They were logically impossible, as Twain's contrasting treatment of Arthur makes only too clear, but in their very impossibility lay their goodness, and in their goodness lay all the goodness of history. In *The Prince and the Pauper* Twain would "account for certain mildnesses which distinguished Edward VI's reign from those that preceded and followed it," not by an appeal to institutions as he did later in *A Connecticut Yankee,* but by bringing innate goodness directly to bear on iniquity.

In the working out of this theme, only the career of Joan of Arc would furnish Twain more ready-made raw materials—more of those historical "facts" he so cherished—than did the short life of Edward VI. David Hume, Twain's chief historical source, describes Edward as possessing "mildness of disposition, application to study and business, a capacity to learn and judge, and an attachment to equity and justice." Hume adds only one qualifier: "He seems only to have contracted, from his education, and from the age in which he lived, too much of a narrow predisposition in matters of religion, which made him incline somewhat to bigotry and persecution." [7] In the personality of Edward VI, in short, a good heart was in conflict with a stultifying conscience. In an earlier passage Hume gives a telling illustration of this conflict. A young woman called Joan Bocher was about to be sent to the stake on an obscure point of heresy until young Edward, who "had more sense than all his counsellors and preceptors," intervened and "refused to sign the warrant for her execution." Only after all sorts of weighty theological arguments were brought

7. *The History of England* (New York, 1880), *3,* 301.

to bear on him did he submit, "though with tears in his eyes" (pp. 267–8).

Here, indeed, was material aplenty for Twain. In *The Prince and the Pauper* he apparently echoes Hume in that scene in which Tom Canty as Edward first really asserts his new and fortuitously won power.[8] Inquiring about a hooting and shouting mob approaching along the road—the mob, here as elsewhere, Twain's most effective symbol of the craven baseness of most human beings—Tom is informed that they are following a man, woman, and young girl to execution. His reaction is immediate and instinctive: "The spirit of compassion took control of him, to the exclusion of all other considerations; he never thought of the offended laws, or of the grief or loss which these criminals had inflicted upon their victims, he could think of nothing but the scaffold and the grisly fate hanging over the heads of the condemned" (*14*, 114–15). This, incidentally, is a paler but more explicit statement of Huck's feelings when he sees the king and duke tarred and feathered: "Well, it made me sick to see it, and I was sorry for them poor pitiful rascals, it seemed like I couldn't even feel any hardness against them any more in the world. It was a dreadful thing to see. Human beings *can* be awful cruel to one another" (*13*, 320–1). But, where Tom can intervene and set right, Huck can only look on and mourn; this is the truest measure of the maturity of the later book.

Before Tom does set things right, however, he almost turns the condemned over to their fate because the evidence of witchcraft against them seems overwhelming and because his mind (again like Huck's) completely accepts the superstitions of his day. Only at the last instant does he

8. The essential situation (aside from the happy ending) of this episode suggests Hume. But Twain's own note (*11*, 278) states that the details concerning the woman who could "rain a storm" by pulling off her stockings comes from F. Hammond Trumbull's *Blue Laws, True and False*, another of his main sources.

save them by the native shrewdness of his questioning—a product, not of his learning, but of his lack of education mingled with his strong grasp of empiric reality and his innate sense of values. These are the same kind of questions which Twain enjoyed putting in the mouth of Nigger Jim and which (when Twain uses the technique for something more than its mechanical joke value) undercut so effectively the dogmas of society.

Edward VI, of course, as befitted a monarch who was to have no parallel before the later nineteenth century, was conceived of by Twain and his sources as a great believer in education. After he has been set upon and beaten by the boys of Christ's Hospital, he resolves that, when he regains power, "they shall not have bread and shelter only, but also teachings out of books; for a full belly is little worth where the mind's starved, and the heart. I will keep this diligently in my remembrance, that this day's lesson be not lost upon me, and my people suffer thereby; for learning softeneth the heart and breedeth gentleness and charity" (*11*, 22).[9] Edward's sentiments here have a certain amount of historical accuracy (as Twain was quick to point out) and what is more important, are completely in accord with Twain's theory of progress. However, it is hard to believe that Edward could have perpetuated these sentiments after his subsequent experiences along the road—all of which seem to point a different moral.[1]

9. It should be noted that Twain by no means indiscriminately idealizes all children. Particularly in mobs, their cruel actions can bear a resemblance to those of their elders which is particularly tragic because it reveals how early the potential for good has been destroyed. One of the most powerful scenes in *A Connecticut Yankee* is that in which the Yankee interrupts some children who are "playing mob" by hanging one of their playmates (*14*, 304).

1. Edward VI was, indeed, the founder of Christ's Hospital as an educational institution. Of course, modern scholarship has attacked Edward's reputation "as a very good boy who had founded schools" (G. M. Trevelyan, *Illustrated English Social History,* London and New York, Longmans, Green,

At the height of Edward's degradation, for example, when he has escaped from the gang of thieves and is walking the roads ragged, lonely, and hungry, he meets rebuffs and curses every time he stops at a farmhouse and asks for help. With a sense of total isolation from the rest of humanity, he stumbles along the road. "All sounds were remote; they made the little king feel that all life and activity were far removed from him, and that he stood solitary, companionless, in the center of a measureless solitude." He finally slips unnoticed into a barn and lies down next to something he soon discovers is a calf. "The king was not only delighted to find that the creature was only a calf," Twain wrote,

> but delighted to have the calf's company; for he had been feeling so lonesome and friendless that the company and comradeship of even this humble animal was welcome. And he had been so buffeted, so rudely entreated by his own kind, that it was a real comfort to him to feel that he was at last in the society of a fellow creature that had at least a soft heart and a gentle spirit, whatever loftier attributes might be lacking. So he resolved to waive rank and make friends with the calf. [*II*, 150–4]

This association of boy and calf—of a child uncorrupted by civilization with a creature beyond its pale—is reminiscent of both the relationship of Huck and Jim and Eve and the animals in Eden. This relationship is the "divine estate" that Satan described to Eve when he told her that whatever she and the animals did was "right and innocent."

Characteristically, Twain's image of man before the Fall

1949, *I*, 108). Twain's sources and Twain himself, as I have noted earlier, searched back through history to find people who possessed, at least in germ, the same beliefs as themselves. Edward's reputation is a fine example of the kind of distortion to which this approach can lead.

is quickly followed by the complementary image of sleep and stasis. After Edward has cuddled up to the calf,

> pleasant thoughts came at once; life took on a cheerfuler seeming. He was free of the bonds of servitude and crime, free of the companionship of base and brutal criminals; he was warm, he was sheltered; in a word, he was happy. The night wind . . . swept by in fitful gusts . . . He merely snuggled the closer to his friend in a luxury of warm contentment and drifted blissfully out of consciousness into a deep and dreamless sleep that was full of serenity and peace. [*11*, 154–5]

Youth, innocence, freedom, and sleep—these ideas and images were inextricably mingled in Twain's consciousness to suggest a mode of existence far removed from the terrors of time and history. That they were somehow related to personal psychological problems seems obvious. He once commented in a revealing note: "I was never old in a dream yet." [2] As major symbols, youth and sleep lie at the very center of Twain's best fiction. Where Edward achieves a momentary freedom with the calf in a barn, Huck flees from the Grangerford feud to Jim and the raft, but the pattern remains the same. "You feel mighty free and easy and comfortable on a raft," says Huck, and there follows an idyll of three days and nights as they drift down the river, go naked (clothes, of course, being one of the prime symbols in the book of the civilization Huck is rejecting), and "watch the lonesomeness of the river, and kind of lazy along and by and by lazy off to sleep." For Huck, "other places do seem so cramped up and smothery, but a raft don't" (*13*, 161–5). The reference to places "cramped up and smothery" is another image of civilization like that of clothes: i.e. houses, institutions, and, by extension, the

2. Notebook 32(I), p. 6.

Page 2

entire system of rigid determinism which constitutes for Twain the "law" of history.

When King Edward awakes on the following morning, he finds himself being stared at by two little girls "with their innocent eyes." Almost without question, they accept his pledge that he is king, and he, in turn, pours out his troubles "where they would not be scoffed at or doubted." Eventually they run to get him food, and the king says to himself: "When I am come to mine own again, I will always honor little children, remembering how that these trusted me and believed in me in my time of trouble; whilst they that were older, and thought themselves wiser, mocked at me and held me for a liar." Twain hammers home this point with particular force when the children's mother receives Edward kindly but pities his "apparently crazed intellect." Even the best and most sympathetic of adults, in short (and these were few and far between), had lost the innocence, the instinctive—and, to the adult, naive—honesty that they were born with (*11*, 156–9). Later in the novel, when Miles Hendon himself is accused of being an impostor, he asks the king if he doubts him, and the king answers immediately, "with a childlike simplicity and faith," that he does not. But to Edward's own question, "dost thou doubt me?" Hendon, the adult, can give no such simple and spontaneous answer (*11*, 202–3).

"I have never written a book for boys; I write for grown ups who have *been* boys," Twain noted late in life.[3] His distinction is a crucial one. The importance of boyhood, Twain seems to be saying, lies not so much in the kind of experiences encountered, as in the way a boy reacts to experience—a way which reflects a complex of values enormously precious to the mature person but undiscoverable in the adult world of time and history. The children who befriended Edward, and Edward himself,

3. Notebook 35 (1902), p. 20.

were as yet almost unmarred by the knowledge of good and evil which would be an inevitable part of their later development. Perhaps the growth of reason would compensate for the loss of innocence and bring about a Utopia greater than the one that had been lost; this has been the dominant hope of Western Society at least since the seventeenth century, a hope predicated squarely on the acceptance of history.[4] With a part of his consciousness Twain, of course, embraced this hope. His Edward, as we have already noted, plans to educate the children of Christ's Hospital, for "learning softeneth the heart and breedeth gentleness and charity." But that part of Twain which rejected the ameliorative influence of history—which, in other words, could no longer accept the theory that history was the vehicle carrying man forward to the new Eden—necessarily rejected all hope.

Individuals of most earlier societies could dream of Eden without predicating their dreams on the forward movement of history. For the ancients the future was the past: Eden would return and then decay again during an infinity of cycles, a more or less mechanical process which, for all practical purposes, annulled time and "abolished" history. Such cyclical theories were essentially optimistic. Catastrophe was normal and certain in meaning because no event was irreversible, no transformation final.[5] For the Western mind, however, nurtured on the concept of one great cycle of Fall and Redemption, cyclical theories (especially as they have been secularized in modern times from cycles of cosmos to those of civilization—not "abolishing" history but simply making it meaningless) are an expression of pessimism and hopelessness. Certainly they are

4. See Arthur O. Lovejoy, *Essays in the History of Ideas* (New York, 1955), pp. 277–95, and Tuveson, *Millennium and Utopia*, pp. 71–201.

5. Mircea Eliade, *The Myth of the Eternal Return* (New York, Pantheon, 1954), pp. 88–9. See also Eliade's entire discussion, pp. 1–102, and Löwith, *Meaning in History*, pp. 3–17.

for Twain, who stresses the endless return of evil—never of Eden. There was only one Eden and that was in the past—in dreams, in fantasy, in the responses of children, in the image of a raft floating down the Mississippi.

Only in *Huckleberry Finn* do the images which express Twain's mature vision fully coalesce and find a style—ultimately a point of view—adequate to express them. A brief examination of some of the weaknesses of *The Prince and the Pauper* will make this fact all the more apparent. We have already noted that as characters King Edward and Tom Canty stand somewhere between Tom Sawyer and Huckleberry Finn. They have all the latter's innate goodness in the face of conscience and social codes but they have to learn his realism. Their instincts are undamaged but, at the beginning of *The Prince and the Pauper,* their vision is clouded by the same chimera of false romance that fills the imagination of Tom Sawyer. It is not so much that Canty and Edward must "learn mercy" as it is that they must learn to distinguish between the real and the make-believe. As the novel opens, each, in his own way, has an utterly false picture of the world of the other: Canty dreams of the status and power of a prince; Edward longs for an urchin's freedom. At the end of the book one has learned about the captivity and the responsibility of rulers; the other, about the depravity and helplessness of the ruled. They have achieved a new awareness which allows them to bring their instinctive sympathies more fully into play. In the final scenes, the goodness and unhappiness of Canty restores Edward to his throne, and he, in turn—now the ideal combination of innate goodness, awareness, and absolute power—dispenses "justice and retribution" to all the wronged and the wrong-doers (*11,* 271–4).

Twain obviously was attempting to have his cake and eat it too. To a figure in time and history he gave values which he was unable to locate in time and history. As a result, Twain not only blurred his conception of history, but failed to project in a credible fashion those values which represented his attempt to escape from its tyranny. Thematically, *The Prince and the Pauper* was true to neither his pessimism nor his optimism; it offered a false diminution of the terrors of history while, at the same time, it distorted the deterministic process of history as Twain officially conceived it. Above all, in *The Prince and the Pauper* Twain failed to develop a concrete image that would suggest a mode of existence sharply differentiated from that of man in history.

On all counts *Huckleberry Finn* resolves the problems raised by the earlier novel. The book, of course, is literally saturated with the nightmare of history, a nightmare nowhere mitigated by the hope of progress. This point has been documented by modern scholarship time and time again.[6] The bigotry and squalor of small town life, "the injustice, the hypocrisy, the general moral ugliness and weakness of Southern society before the war," [7] the false and vicious romanticism of Walter Scott, the perverted values of the entire feudal tradition—all find a place in the panorama of history presented by Twain in *Huckleberry Finn.* Because the time of the action was set securely in the past (unlike the situation in *Life on the Mississippi* where the description of social change required interpretive comment) and because his hero was a social outcast rather than a boy king identified with liberal politics, Twain had

6. See, e.g., De Voto, *Mark Twain at Work,* pp. 87–104; Edgar M. Branch, "The Two Providences: Thematic Form in *Huckleberry Finn," College English, 11* (1950), 190–1, and, especially, Richard P. Adams, "The Unity and Coherence of *Huckleberry Finn," Tulane Studies in English, 6* (1956), 92–5. Walter Blair has exhaustively explored this subject in *Mark Twain and Huck Finn.* Especially significant is his revelation that Twain's reading in history and historical novels pervades even the plot situations of the book.

7. Adams, p. 94.

neither to commit himself on the direction of historical movement nor palliate the evils of the past with miraculous interventions. In *Huckleberry Finn* his historical vision could merge effortlessly with his vision of the baseness of human nature; entirely absent is the tension between the two so characteristic of much of his writing.

But in *Huckleberry Finn* as in *Life on the Mississippi* time stops at the water's edge. Describing his trip down the great river by steamboat in 1882, Twain wrote that on the Mississippi "the day goes, the night comes, and again the day—and still the same, night after night and day after day—majestic, unchanging sameness of serenity, repose, tranquillity, lethargy, vacancy—symbol of eternity, realization of the heaven pictured by priest and prophet" (*12*, 225). On this particular occasion the mood of serenity depressed him, probably because it reflected the present "lonesomeness" of the Mississippi caused by the absence of the colorful fleets of shipping remembered from his youth. At other times Twain reacted very differently to similar experiences. In *A Tramp Abroad,* for example, he tells what it is like to float down the Neckar: "The motion of a raft . . . is gentle, and gliding, and smooth, and noiseless: it calms down all feverish activities, it soothes to sleep all nervous hurry and impatience; under its restful influence all the troubles and vexations and sorrows that harass the mind vanish away, and existence becomes a dream, a charm, a deep and tranquil ecstasy" (*11*, 107). Here again the images of sleep and of motion over water coalesce to become a symbol of peace, security, stasis, but here, in addition, they are welcomed as a form of mystical release that annuls the agony of consciousness. Twain seems at least half-aware that his symbolism is close to that of traditional mythology, where the image of sleep is often used to describe the arrival of the hero into complete communion with the divine world. Here he exists in bliss, beholding only immutable forms, above change and death and time, above earthly pain and joy, while "eon after eon of earthly history rolls by." [8]

A decade later, in his sketch "Down the Rhone," Twain returned to the attractions of the floating raft. It afforded repose, he said, "all the while out of reach of the news and remote from the world and its concerns"; at the same time, he noted the "noiseless motion . . . the strange absence of the sense of sin, and the stranger absence of the desire to commit it" (*29*, 129, 139). The raft, in this case, is described as offering release from the moral sense—the curse of Adam, the burden of man in history. "Land, I warn't in no hurry to git out and buck at civilization again," says Huck as he drifts along in a balloon in *Tom Sawyer Abroad* (1894); and he goes on to explain: "Now one of the worst things about civilization is, that anybody that gits a letter with trouble in it comes and tells you all about it and makes you feel bad, and the newspapers fetches you the troubles of everybody all over the world, and keeps you downhearted and dismal 'most all the time, and it is such a heavy load for a person" (*29*, 58). Neither freedom nor happiness, in short, could be found on land, in time and history.

These examples of a recurrent symbol are valuable chiefly as they shed light on the meaning of *Huckleberry Finn;* in the context of the works in which they are found they remain undeveloped and largely functionless. *Huckleberry Finn,* indeed, is an artistic triumph precisely because, in this one book, Twain's dream of Eden has organic meaning as the single moral and spiritual alternative to the unmitigated terrors of civilization. At the same time, this dream is given substance, made vivid and palpable, by linking the image of childhood with both the image of

8. Joseph Campbell, *The Hero with a Thousand Faces* (New York, Meridian, 1956), pp. 218–23.

the raft and raftsmen and the image of the pilot. Twain himself, it should be noted, was at least half-conscious of these identifications and of their significance. When he transferred to *Life on the Mississippi* the flyting episode originally in *Huckleberry Finn,* he introduced his pirated materials by telling about the hero of his new novel—an ignorant boy who has run away from a "persecuting good widow who wishes to make a nice, truth-telling, respectable boy of him" and who floats down the river on "a fragment of a lumber raft" (*12,* 19). Huck shares with the raftsmen their joyousness, their profound antipathy to organized society, their essential honesty and generosity and loyalty (as opposed to the repeated violations of trust and brotherhood—to the systematic chicanery and faithlessness—of those grotesque parodies of civilized man, the King and the Duke).

Huck and the raftsmen seem literally to have some of the qualities of demigods—seem, in other words, to be related to forces elemental, profound, anterior to civilization. Twain suggests this superbly in the ritual boasting of the Child of Calamity:

> when I'm thirsty I reach up and suck the cloud dry like a sponge; when I range the earth hungry, famine follows in my tracks! Whoo-oop! Bow your neck and spread! . . . The massacre of isolated communities is the pastime of my idle moments, the destruction of nationalities the serious business of my life! The boundless vastness of the great American desert is my enclosed property, and I bury my dead on my own premises! [*12,* 22]

The primitive, vital, and distinctly anarchic power of the American wilderness hero has nowhere been better expressed than in the grotesque challenges and tall tales of the rivermen. As Constance Rourke has noted: "It was the wilderness with its impenetrable depths, the wild storms of the West, the great rivers, the strange new wonders on every side, that produced the content of the stories—those natural elements that had brought terror and suffering to earlier pioneers . . . but now were apprehended with an insurgent comic rebound and a consciousness of power."[9] Certainly this power is the ultimate source of Huck's composure, his passion for freedom, and his hedonism. One is reminded of the scene in which he and Jim huddle around a fire in a cave eating while a tremendous thunderstorm rages outside and Mississippi overflows its banks and of his remark on this occasion: "Jim, this is nice . . . I wouldn't want to be nowhere else but here. Pass me along another hunk of fish and some hot cornbread" (*13*, 68).

Twain's mature vision, it must be stressed, embodies both a passive and an active principle. If a dream of peace and joy and comradeship lies at the very center of this vision, it is nevertheless true that the capacity for independent moral *action* clings to the periphery. Behind Huck lurks the image not only of the raftsmen but the pilot. Again the association was almost explicit in Twain's mind. In his *Autobiography* he points out that Huck was drawn from his childhood playmate, Tom Blankenship, and he added by way of comment on Tom: "He was the only really independent person—boy or man—in the community, and by consequence he was tranquilly and continually happy, and was envied by all the rest of us" (*37*, 174). The resemblance in phrasing between this passage and the one in *Life on the Mississippi* in which the pilot is described as "the only unfettered and entirely independent human being that lived in the earth" (*12*, 18) clearly suggests the identification made by Twain of Huck (or Tom Blankenship) with all that the pilots stood for in his mind. The

9. *American Humor*, p. 49.

hint of another river story in one of Twain's notebooks of this period offers further evidence of how closely he linked Huck with the pilot-house: "Make a kind of Huck Finn narrative on a boat—let him ship as cabin boy & another boy as cub pilot—& so put the great river & its bygone ways into history in the form of a story." [1]

Although Huck is disinherited, rootless, undisciplined (a "cabin boy" not an actual "cub"), he nevertheless shares something of the pilots' fundamental sobriety and tough incisiveness, their capacity for swift action based on a realistic appraisal of the facts. At the same time his power—the potential Promethean thrust of his personality—is tempered as the Yankee's is not by a vivid sense of human limitations before the immutability of nature and circumstances. Like the pilots, Huck has no time "to be sentimentering" (*13*, 98), whether he is groping in the dark for the ship's boat after the raft has broken loose from the *Walter Scott;* or evaluating the King and the Duke ("It didn't take me long to make up my mind that these liars warn't no kings nor dukes at all, but just low-down humbugs and frauds. But I never said nothing . . . then . . . you don't get into no trouble" [*13*, 174]); or coming to understand the humanity of Jim ("I do believe he cared just as much for his people as white folks does for their'n. It don't seem natural but I reckon it's so" [*13*, 215]). "I reckon it's so": it is this honest recognition of the facts that is behind Huck's climactic moral decision. He thinks back; he *sees* Jim's many acts of love; and then characteristically makes a rapid decision based on what he has seen. A moment later finds him busy translating decision into deeds: "Then I set to thinking over how to get at it [i.e. stealing Jim out of slavery again] . . . and at last fixed up a plan that suited me" (*13*, 206–7).

In Huck, Twain portrayed an individual who acted,

1. Notebook 18 (1883–84), p. 21.

not from convictions (the prejudices of civilized man), but from acute perceptions, native intelligence, and a warm heart. "He was as tough and practical as the pilot," says Leo Marx, "and as sensitive to color and line as an artist; he kept his eye on dangerous snags, but he did not lose his sense of the river's loveliness." [2] In other words, Twain found in Huckleberry Finn a point of view that could encompass at once the real beauty as well as the terror and sham of human experience. Not that Huck is without his aesthetic blind-spots (seen, for example, in his admiration of the Grangerford house). These are, however, like his conscience and the physical invasion of the raft by the King and the Duke: symbols of a civilization that constantly impinges on without corrupting or destroying him. Even in the Grangerford living-room his merciless realism constantly impells him toward an evaluation that it is simply beyond his sophistication to make. In any case, we are never long unaware of the real glories that Huck has seen and felt, and these give Twain a vivid background on which to cast in high relief the more naive opinions of his protagonist.

Between them, Huck and Jim are related to the demigods of the river, to the barbarous primitivism of the Negro, and beyond that, to the archetypal primitives of the Golden Age, instinctively good, uncorrupted by reason, living close to nature and more influenced by its portents than by the conventions of civilization.[3] Tom Sawyer, by way of contrast, is always associated with history; Huck says of him in *Tom Sawyer Abroad* that "he just dripped history from every pore" (*19,* 111). A recent critic has described Tom with equal aptness as "the romantic working within the

2. "The Pilot and the Passenger," p. 142.

3. For an exhaustive examination of the meaningful role of superstition in the lives of Huck and Jim see Ray W. Frantz, Jr., "The Role of Folklore in *Huckleberry Finn,*" *American Literature,* 27 (1956), 314–27.

accepted social and moral framework." [4] His romanticism, indeed, is the false romanticism of the South where (so Twain argued in *Life on the Mississippi*) the worst cruelties of history were covered over with a thin veneer of glamour and sentimentality and made into codes—what we might term "rituals of civilization" in contrast to the vital natural rituals of Huck and Jim and the raftsmen. It is, of course, these rituals of civilization that are parodied by Twain in the opening as well as the final scenes of the book.

In short, here as elsewhere in *Huckleberry Finn* myth and history are forced into sharp juxtaposition; and it is from the disparity between these two modes of being that the larger meanings of the book emerge. Five years later in *A Connecticut Yankee,* Twain would suggest a solution that was entirely within the context of history to the problem of evil in history. But in *Huckleberry Finn* this problem is countered (not resolved—this was the mistake of *The Prince and the Pauper*) by the dream of Eden. Myths do not deny the agony of man in time: rather, "they reveal within, behind, and around it essential peace." [5] Twain all his life longed for this peace and sought to give his longings artistic expression. "When it was dark," says Huck, "I set by my campfire smoking and feeling pretty satisfied, but by and by it got sort of lonesome, and so I went and set on the bank and listened to the current swashing along and counted the stars and drift-logs and rafts that come down and then went to bed; there ain't no better way to put in time when you are lonesome; you can't stay so, you soon get over it" (*13,* 54). Myths, necessarily, are merely concrete representations of the ineffable. Only in the image of the flowing river and the boy who communes with it did Twain convincingly succeed in describing a mode of being apart from the tyranny of history.

4. Branch, p. 193.
5. Campbell, p. 288.

8.

THE COSMIC WOMAN: *Joan of Arc*

> There is in myth a perpetual theme, in the voices of the prophets a familiar cry. The people yearn for some personality who, in a world of twisted bodies and souls, will represent again the lines of the incarnate image. We are familiar with the myth from our own tradition. It occurs everywhere, under a variety of guises. When the Herod figure (the extreme symbol of misgoverning, tenacious ego) has brought mankind to the nadir of spiritual abasement, the occult forces of the cycle begin of themselves to move. In an inconspicuous village the maid is born who will maintain herself undefiled of the fashionable errors of her generation: a miniature in the midst of men of the cosmic woman who was the bride of the wind.
>
> Campbell, *The Hero with the Thousand Faces*

For Mark Twain as for many other individuals of the eighteenth and nineteenth centuries faith in history was a substitute for faith in God. But Twain's was always a tenuous faith—tormented by a dream of freedom and innocence outside the grip of time, shaken by his abiding sense of human sinfulness, and finally destroyed by personal suffering and a growing awareness of the oligarchic and imperialistic drift of America. We have had occasion to note that even *A Connecticut Yankee in King Arthur's Court,* ostensibly Twain's most belligerent assertion of the moral and material progress of Western Civilization, is a deeply ambivalent book and ultimately an artistic failure because of its ambivalence. It is a novel in which the conscious intentions of the author are at cross purposes with his most deeply felt imaginative insights. The unresolved and largely unacknowledged ambiguities of the *Connecticut Yankee* became, under the stresses of the 90's, the intellectual problems with which Twain was to wrestle for the rest of his life. On the one hand, he attempted to develop a cyclical theory of history. On the other, he was more and more driven to escape imaginatively from the nightmarish implications of his own rational formulations. *Joan of Arc* can be most fruitfully examined as a final, desperate attempt to establish values apart from the futile treadmill of sin and suffering which constituted the life of man on earth.

For Joan, Twain felt none of the mixed emotions which had characterized his attitude toward the Yankee. He revered her, and, according to Paine, this reverence led him during the winter of 1893 to write her biography with a concentration and dedication almost unparalleled in the rest of his work. "This is to be a serious book," he told Livy and Susy in explanation of the fact that he was writing it anonymously. "It means more to me than anything I have ever undertaken" (*32,* 959). With more justice than he was perhaps aware of, an early reviewer of *Joan of Arc* observed that "devotion running into idolatry is the burden of his song." [1]

Twain had chosen a propitious subject for his idolatry. The story of Joan of Arc—at once strong in outline, vague in many of its details, dramatic in its historical consequences, and romantic with its young heroine—calls forth

1. Charles W. Colby, "The Maid of Orleans," *Nation, 63* (1896), 53.

endless interpreters, each of whom reveals as much about himself as about Joan. Indeed, the variety of literary treatment to which Joan's life has been subjected seems to suggest, if not that all historical writing is contemporary, at least that it contains a strong subjective element. To the nineteenth century, particularly, Joan appeared especially fascinating and especially baffling. Lacking in either a complete and unbiased picture of her life or an adequate understanding of the Middle Ages, it conceived of her as a glorious enigma. To study Joan was, at least in part, to renounce the rule of reason, to admit exceptions to the laws of strict causality. It is this quality of uniqueness in the life of Joan that Twain stresses again and again in writing about her. The personality which made possible her amazing career, he says in an article called "St. Joan of Arc," "is one to be reverently studied, loved, and marveled at, but not to be wholly understood and accounted for by even the most searching analysis." "The measure of their talent does not explain the whole result of the lives of other geniuses," Twain goes on to point out. Rather, "it is the atmosphere in which the talent was cradled that explains; it is the training which it received while it grew." But Joan's qualities "became immediately usable and effective without the developing forces of a sympathetic atmosphere and the training which comes of teaching, study, practice." In short,

> out of a cattle pasturing peasant village lost in the remoteness of an unvisited wilderness and atrophied with ages of stupefaction and ignorance we cannot see a Joan of Arc issue equipped to the last detail for her amazing career and hope to be able to explain the riddle of it, labor at it as we may.
>
> It is beyond us. All the rules fail in this girl's case. In the world's history she stands alone—quite alone. [22, 363–4]

Thus does Twain define the historical problem presented by the Joan of Arc story, and his definition is scarcely more extreme, on the whole, than that of other nineteenth-century commentators. Even the great Michelet, while he makes a perfunctory attempt to relate certain facets of Joan's life (e.g. her visions and her taking up arms) to her social background, ends his account of her in a burst of romantic and patriotic ardor; she is a "living enigma," a "phenomenon," a "marvel," a "mysterious creature." [2] Her Catholic biographers, of course, whom Twain read and from whom he occasionally borrowed source material, were authorized by their faith to abandon the yardstick of rationality completely and consequently make Twain and Michelet—even the sentimental popularizer Janet Tuckey—appear models of scientific rectitude.

One cause of the historical dilemma that Twain and others found themselves in was the fact that they were all unconsciously dealing with a radically one-sided image of Joan of Arc. The more amateurish historians among them even felt that a strength of their case lay in the objectivity of the evidence. Twain, for example, wrote, in an introductory note to his book, that "the details of the life of Joan of Arc form a biography which is unique among the world's biographies in one respect: *It is the only story of a human life which comes to us under oath* . . . The history of no other life of that remote time is known with either the certainty or the comprehensiveness that attaches to hers" (*17*, xxi). Actually, according to Charles Lightbody, the facts of her life come to us strained through the sieve of French patriotic sentiment. The nineteenth-century Joan, the Joan of modern French historians and most American writing, is a creation of Armagnac tradition, "clerical, conservative or monarchist, nationalist or romantic." The Joan of this tradition is "a sweet, saintly her-

2. *The Life of Joan of Arc* (New York, 1887), pp. 6, 92.

oine, combining the utmost in feminine charm, humanity and sensibility with the utmost in achievement in the most characteristically masculine realm." On the other hand, the Joan of the realistic Burgundian chroniclers (among them Monstrelet and the "Bourgeois de Paris")—a sort of virago—was lost with the Burgundian cause. Much of Joan's testimony at her trial, Lightbody goes on to point out, is highly dubious and her Rehabilitation (here he echoes Shaw), a complete whitewash. Moreover, with regard to what Twain considered the crucial problem of training, Lightbody notes that there is a good deal of evidence to show that Joan was trained both in horsemanship and in arms. "To suppose," he says, "that the sweet, home-dwelling Maid of most modern biographers is suddenly transformed into the Joan of history is to suppose an absolute impossibility." [3] But this is just the supposition that even rationalists like Michelet and Twain were forced to make on the strength of the apparent evidence. Their only real alternative was to invert the romantic, heroic image completely and produce, like Anatole France, a skeptical and debunking picture of Joan as a sort of army mascot or burlesque her story completely as did Voltaire and turn it into an attack on French monarchical institutions—a step which for emotional and subjective reasons they were unwilling to take.

The liberal and anticlerical Michelet responded to the clerical and monarchist image of Joan of Arc because, as an ardent patriot, he saw her (correctly) as the incarnation of the French national tradition. To Michelet's nationalism Twain, naturally, was far from responsive, though he ends his novel in a burst of rhetoric about Joan as the symbol of Patriotism, presumably a plausible enough sentiment for

3. "Joan of Arc as Her Enemies Saw Her," in *The World of History*, ed. Courtland Canby and Nancy E. Gross (New York, The New American Library, 1954), pp. 190–4.

de Conte. Twain's official theme rings particularly hollow, however, if we keep in mind not only his lifelong dislike of the French nation, but the actual fact that the "Conclusion" to the "Joan of Arc" manuscript in the Mark Twain Papers is written in the black ink Twain was using for revisions (as opposed to the bluish-purple ink of the original text). It seems safe to assume, therefore, that this conclusion was an afterthought designed to round out the book and give it some kind of positive meaning. The original text ends with Joan at the stake. Certainly for Michelet's occasional chauvinism Twain had nothing but contempt. In the margin of his own copy of *The Life of Joan of Arc,* for example, opposite Michelet's comment that an English or German woman would not have risked the journey from Vaucouleurs to Chinon because of the "indelicacy of the proceeding," Twain remarked: "How stupid! A *Joan of Arc* would do it no matter *what* her nationality might be. That spirit has no nationality." [4] The equally liberal and anticlerical Twain responded to the prevalent image of Joan both because she appealed to his romantic ideal of womanhood and for far deeper and more complex reasons, some of which we shall explain in the course of this chapter.

Whatever their motives, both writers were thus essentially committed to the solution of an historical problem which Twain at least freely admitted was rationally insoluble. Yet the whole matter is further complicated by the fact that, granted the traditional Joan was a one-sided picture, neither author could really relate even this Joan to the Middle Ages because neither author understood the Middle Ages in the sense that any historian must "understand" a given period in order to interpret it correctly—that is, by being able to re-experience or relive it sympa-

4. Paris, 1873, p. 20; MTP.

thetically in his own mind.[5] Edmund Wilson in *To the Finland Station* points out that Michelet was more interested in Joan as having established the "modern type of hero of action 'contrary to passive Christianity' " than in Joan as a mystic. Concerning his attitude toward the Middle Ages in general, Wilson notes that "what Michelet really admires are not the virtues which the chivalrous and Christian centuries cultivated but the heroisms of the scientist and the artist, the Protestant in religion and politics, the efforts of man to understand his situation and rationally to control his development." [6] But Michelet's *History of the Middle Ages* is at least a qualified success because, even when his inspiration and sympathy fail him, he can still count on his vast erudition and his considerable knowledge of social and economic processes to carry the day.

Unfortunately such is not the case with Twain, whose formal learning was slight, whose concept of institutions is symbolized in the easily built and easily destroyed "man-factories" of the Yankee, and whose hatred of most aspects of medieval life was as virulent as that of Voltaire. Herbert Muller has noted the peculiar tendency of the Middle Ages to continually engender historical fiction "as later generations were charmed by their ideal theory or repelled by their barbarous practice." [7] Twain was largely ignorant of medieval theory and what he knew—or thought he knew—of it clashed, of course, with his Enlightenment ideals. With medieval practices he was equally horrified. As a result, he could not relate his image of Joan of Arc to his image of the Middle Ages. How, indeed, was one to explain the impossibly good in terms of the impossibly bad?

5. See Collingwood, *The Idea of History*, p. 327.
6. New York, Doubleday (1953), pp. 9–10.
7. *The Uses of the Past* (New York, New American Library, 1954), p. 233.

Joan was as unique morally as she was in her untrained genius. "When we reflect," he remarks in his preface, "that her century was the brutalest, the wickedest, the rottenest in history since the darkest ages, we are lost in wonder at the miracle of such a product from such a soil. The contrast between her and her century is the contrast between day and night" (*17*, xxi). Joan's innate goodness was clearly a miraculous phenomenon. Twain had written an historical novel whose protagonist was historically meaningless because outside the web of historical causality.

Certain of his Catholic sources were actually on far surer logical grounds when they treated Joan's story frankly as a saint's tale and derived from it a theological meaning, yet it was these very writers whom Twain mocked most unmercifully for their credulity in his marginal comments to their works. "This in the 19th century," he sneered at Monsignor Richard's suggestion that the Archangel Michael personally intervened in a battle. On another occasion, Richard related an incident in which Joan's saints refused to give her advice, and Twain noted marginally: "These saints are merely idiots. They remind her of nothing that is valuable." [8] For the more sentimental and pietistic Countess de Chabannes, he had even harsher strictures. When she attempted to explain Joan's success and popularity with the common people by arguing that it is the privilege of the poor to recognize more easily those whom God sends because "where He chooses His instruments, He also provides witnesses" Twain was quick to spot the absurdity. Beside the passage he wrote: "It seems so great and wonderful that he should choose his instruments by preference among the dull and ignorant that I marvel He does not choose cats—His glory would be the greater and the argument is the same." [9] Twain, in short, ridiculed

8. *Jeanne d'Arc, La Vénérable* (Paris, n.d.), pp. 23, 213–34; MTP.
9. *La Vierge Lorraine, Jeanne d'Arc* (Paris, 1890), p. 39; MTP.

miraculous explanations to certain problems he had himself defined as miraculous. His rationalism and deep-seated dislike of Catholicism prevented him from any easy recourse to traditional Christian interpretations of the Joan "riddle." We shall, nevertheless, observe later how close he actually came to the essential Catholic position on Joan.

It was on Catholicism, of course, that Twain had centered his attack in *A Connecticut Yankee;* the Roman Church in that earlier book emerges as the prime mover of all evil in history since the fall of Rome. Such a sweeping assumption, which Twain had by no means abandoned in the 90's, made it scarcely conceivable that his adored heroine should have taken an active part in the religious life of the Middle Ages. When, for example, the Countess de Chabannes describes Joan as confessing herself several times to the Franciscans at Neufchateau during the two weeks she was there in her youth, Twain noted marginally: "Think of this heroic soul in such company—and yet nothing but this base superstition could lift her to that fearless height." [1] Joan's later conflict with "this base superstition," however, Twain could comprehend and passionately sympathize with, especially since the perfect villain was at hand in the person of the Bishop of Beauvais.

Inevitably for Twain and other nineteenth-century biographers and historians of the Protestant and rationalist tradition the deeply equivocal figure of Pierre Cauchon—apparently the very incarnation of the base, subtle, and Machiavellian priest—represented a heaven-sent opportunity for the expression of anti-clerical sentiments. Even Catholic writers after the Rehabilitation were authorized to throw him to the dogs with scant explanation. For a villain condemned so unanimously Twain naturally would listen to no extenuating pleas. To the rash suggestion of one of his sources that Cauchon did not act with deliberate

1. Ibid., p. 25.

iniquity, Twain contemptuously scrawled "Shucks" across the margin of the page.[2] De Conte certainly speaks for his creator when he describes the Bishop as "the cruelest man and the most shameless that has lived in this world" (*18*, 133). Cauchon, accordingly, emerges in the novel a caricature of absolute evil. "When I looked at that obese president," says de Conte at the beginning of the trial, "puffing and wheezing there, his great belly distending and receding with each breath, and noted his three chins, fold above fold, and his knobby and knotty face, and his purple and splotchy complexion, and his repulsive cauliflower nose, and his cold and malignant eyes—a brute every detail of him—my heart sank." In contrast to this monster, Joan enters the court "a dainty little figure . . . gentle and innocent . . . winning and beautiful in the fresh bloom of her seventeen years" (*18*, 123–4). Twain is dealing entirely in stereotypes here; the Armagnac image of Joan and the Protestant image of the fat and lecherous priest merge imperceptibly into the heroine and villain of Victorian popular literature. We are asked to cheer as time and time again the frail but indomitable virgin foils the vile seducer. The diction takes on the overtones of domestic melodrama. "One wonders if he [Cauchon] ever knew his mother or ever had a sister," the agonized de Conte thinks on one occasion (*18*, 223); on another, after Cauchon and his cohorts bore a hole in Joan's cell to hear her confessions: "One wonders how they could treat that poor child so. She had not done them any harm" (*18*, 223). Twain's abysmal ignorance of the historical forces at work in the Middle Ages is never more clearly revealed than in this last remark of de Conte; he had reduced a death struggle between political and social systems to the Victorian convention of the female in distress. De Conte, of course, is the hero of the melodrama, prevented from rescuing the heroine at the point of his

2. John O'Hagan, *Joan of Arc* (London, 1893), p. 68; MTP.

sword by the awkward facts of history. A note inside the cover of the Countess de Chabannes' biography suggests that Twain at one time planned to have several of Joan's playmates make an *attempted* rescue.

Melodrama, polarization of character, loss of meaning are some of the results of the idealization of Joan, or, in other words, the basic inability of Twain and other nineteenth- and often twentieth-century writers to relate Joan to her environment. As Bernard Shaw succinctly put it: "If you are quite convinced that the world has progressed enormously, both morally and mechanically, since Joan's time, then you will never understand why Joan was burnt, much less feel that you might have voted for burning her yourself . . . and until you feel that you know nothing essential about her." [3]

It remains for us to pursue further some of the implications and ramifications of Twain's idealization. If Joan's genius had flowered without training, if her moral values were antithetical to those of her brutal environment, she must have been above the pleasure-pain psychology and free from the moral sense that Twain felt to be characteristic of the human mind. Thus she was truly unselfish, in Twain's words, "perhaps the only entirely unselfish person whose name has a place in profane history" (*17*, xxii). She was a double miracle: unique not only for the Middle Ages but for all time, "the most extraordinary person the human race has ever produced" (*17*, 383). The next step was inevitable. From his Catholic sources (if he did not develop the idea independently) Twain perceived the similarity of Joan to Jesus, of her trial before Cauchon with that of Jesus before the Sanhedrin and Pilate. Above the page in which Monsignor Richard made this explicit comparison

3. *Nine Plays* (New York, Dodd, Mead, 1947), p. 1007. The melodramatic elements have also been noted by Albert E. Stone, Jr., "Mark Twain's *Joan of Arc:* The Child as Goddess," *American Literature, 31* (1959), 11–13.

Twain wrote in bad French: "Il y avait un charge réel contre J.C.—qu'il avait se nommé le roi des Juifs, n'est ce pas? On ne pouvait pas l'eprouver; neaumoins on a-t-il condamnè[.] L'Eglise n'apportait pas contre Jeanne que des soupçonnes et manquèe les établir." [4] Twain seems to be saying that actually the Sanhedrin had a better case against Jesus when they turned him over to Pilate than did the Ecclesiastical Court against Joan when they released her to Warwick. By implication she was more historically "innocent"—more "unselfish" and less caught up in remorseless causality. As Twain put it in another place: "No vestige or suggestion of self-seeking can be found in any word or deed of hers" (*17*, xxii). But it is unwise and unnecessary for us to labor this hint of Joan's superiority to Jesus. What is important to note is that Twain consciously made the comparison, that, in fact, the two images tended to blend in his mind.

A case in point is Joan's trial at Poitiers. Twain, naturally, did not limit the expression of his distaste for Catholicism merely to attacks on the Bishop of Beauvais and his associates; they were simply the most vulnerable targets. For the clerics at Poitiers Twain had only slightly less contempt. His feelings are clear enough from the savage little notes written in his copy of the Countess de Chabannes' *La Vierge Lorraine,* apparently his chief source for the facts of this episode. "Persecution by these mitred donkeys," he scribbled at the head of the Countess de Chabannes' chapter describing the inquiry or, again, further on: "There the question wasn't 'Can this soldier win victories,' but 'Is he a sound Catholic' " (pp. 58, 63). In

4. *Jeanne d'Arc,* p. 167. On the front fly-leaf of Countess de Chabannes' biography Twain wrote:

"Several great historical trials:
Christ before Pilate
Joan's two trials
That man in the time of Mary (?)"

the finished book this idea was given to the supposedly medieval Sieur de Conte and elaborated on in the course of his comments on the scene at Poitiers (*17*, 160).

More significant than Twain's gibes at the Church as an institution, however, is the manner in which on this occasion he borrowed directly from the Countess the religious overtones that continually color her description of Joan of Arc and, in particular, her implied comparison of Joan with Christ. "Assise sur un banc," wrote the Countess, "Jeanne était là devant ses interrogateurs, répondant, sans se troubler, à toutes leurs questions, déconcertant la science de tous ces sages par sa sublime ignorance" (p. 59). Twain underlined this sentence from the word "déconcertant" to the word "ignorance" and later apparently copied the underlined part without change into his own manuscript. Altering the rest of the sentence slightly, he also added a final elaboration. His version of this scene runs as follows:

> She sat there, solitary on her bench, untroubled, and disconcerted the science of the sages with her sublime ignorance—an ignorance which was a fortress; arts, wiles, the learning drawn from books, and all like missiles rebounded from its unconscious masonry and fell to the ground harmless; they could not dislodge the garrison which was within—Joan's serene great heart and spirit. [*17*, 160–1]

The Countess de Chabannes' description of Joan before the tribunal at Poitiers was clearly, as Twain noted in the margin of her book, "Christ before the doctors again" (p. 59). It was this description he chose to borrow almost intact. While rejecting the external trappings of the Catholic position regarding Joan, Twain had, in fact, like the Catholic writers, undertaken to explain her riddle by resorting to that strand of anti-intellectualism and primitivism that is such a pervasive part of Christianity. Devoid of formal training, Joan apparently derived her strength from intuitional and mystical sources—"this intoxicated child," as Twain called her in another note (p. 58). A divine spirit come to dwell among men, she was, like Christ, the more engaging because she consented to be so human. In *La Vierge Lorraine* Twain wrote after one of Joan's exchanges with her examiners: "Good incident[.] Childish but can be improved." Then he added at the bottom of the page: "No, don't improve her poor little sallies—they show what a natural human she was, and she is the more engaging for it" (p. 60). Twain's Joan is clearly a saint but, like the saints of most baffled rationalists, denatured and divorced from teleological ends.

While almost all of Joan's nineteenth-century biographers were forced by the apparent evidence to generally similar conclusions, many of them made heroic attempts to relate the ideal Joan to her base environment before falling into the attitude of awe and wonder that is called forth by the presence of the Divine. Twain, on the other hand, tries to evade the whole historical problem through the use of a narrator. With Twain, the first person point of view is a means of expressing appropriate homage to a saint without taking responsibility for the implications of such homage, just as in *A Connecticut Yankee* it is a means of espousing the idea of progress and at the same time keeping it at arm's length. He might have regarded Joan of Arc simultaneously with a medieval and a modern mind as life on the Mississippi in *Huckleberry Finn* is viewed simultaneously with a boy's and an adult's mind. Instead Twain *alternates* between a medieval and modern point of view as the occasion seems to demand, while always apparently speaking in the voice of de Conte. Thus, for example, de Conte is thoroughly medieval in describing how he actually *saw* St. Michael appear to Joan (*17*, 67–76) and, on the other hand, thoroughly modern in his attack on the priests at Poitiers.[5] Occasionally Twain attempts the kind of irony that might have artistically unified the two visions, but he does this only in order to exploit a humorous situation, never to give meaning to a serious one. De Conte is treated ironically, for example, when he is telling about the dragon that lived in the forest behind Domremy. Nobody has ever seen this dragon, but de Conte confidently describes it as having "a body as big around as a tierce and scales like overlapping great tiles, and deep ruby eyes as large as a cavalier's hat, and an anchor fluke on its tail as big as I don't know what, but very big, even unusually so for a dragon, as everybody said who knew about dragons" (*17*, 7–8). When de Conte describes his dealings with Joan of Arc, however, Twain fails to maintain the same ironic detachment, and the reader accordingly loses all sense of perspective. How are we to evaluate such scenes as the one previously mentioned in which de Conte actually comes upon St. Michael talking to Joan? The gap between Twain and his narrator has closed to such an extent that we are forced to accept the incident at close to its face value. Where the fictive elements in an historical novel should heighten and sharpen the meaning of obscure events—ideally give them both a temporal and a universal significance—those elements in *Joan of Arc* tend to obscure or blur meaning. As an early reviewer pointed out, Twain is forced to commit himself where a cautious historian would hold back.[6] But he commits himself to no good purpose except to abandon the whole historical problem. When we begin to read how de Conte saw "a *white* shadow

5. A Catholic priest, Edward G. Rosenberger, "An Agnostic Hagiographer," *Catholic World, 127* (1928), 717–23, claims Twain created in his description of Joan's vision an "accurately imagined mysticism." Rosenberger points out (though for a different purpose) what I have been stressing in this chapter—namely, the essential similarity of Twain's position to that of the Catholics regarding Joan of Arc.

6. James W. Thompson, "The Maid of Orleans," *Dial, 20* (1896), 355.

[i.e. St. Michael; the italics are Twain's] come slowly gliding along the grass toward the Tree," we are far from the Twain who thought that Joan's saints were "merely idiots" or that one was a fool if one still imagined in the nineteenth century that St. Michael had intervened in French battles. The two positions seem hopelessly disparate and Twain, unlike some of his contemporaries, made no attempt to reconcile them.

If irony was inadmissible in dealing with Joan, so was the kind of direct anachronistic commentary that occasionally elsewhere in the book makes de Conte a mere spokesman for Twain. In revising his text for publication, Twain crossed out the following lines, which were to come after the passage (*17*, 232) in which de Conte argues that the professors at the University of Paris (who had just pronounced Joan's voices to be fiends) might as easily be deceived as Joan: "Privately, I myself never had a high opinion of Joan's voices—I mean in some respects—but that they were devils I do not believe. I think they were saints, holy and pure and well-meaning, but with the saint's natural incapacity for business. Whatever a saint is, he is not clever. There are acres of history to prove it." This is on manuscript pages 341–2. Page 343 is missing but de Conte's comments continue on page 344: ". . . The voices meant Joan nothing but good, and I am sure they did the very best they could with their equipment; but I also feel sure that if they had let her alone her matters would sometimes have gone much better. Remember, these things which I have been saying are privacies—let them go no further; for I have not more desire to be damned than another." Twain obviously realized that the tone and sentiments of this passage, notwithstanding the final sentence, were inappropriate to de Conte. At the same time, they suggest Twain's own skepticism regarding the supernatural aspects of Joan's career and the care which he took to exclude this skepticism from his book because it had so little relation to what he felt about Joan as an individual. What was really important (and what he desperately needed to believe in) was the basic irrationality of her life.

It is not surprising that Twain probably got the initial hint for his description of St. Michael from the Countess de Chabannes (p. 20). Much as he mocked his Catholic sources, he adopted their dominant tone of reverence for Joan as a saint; and while he was fortunately incapable of the Countess de Chabannes' lachrymosity and sentimental and religious effusions (she was, in many ways, a sort of Catholic Emmeline Grangerford), he was nevertheless careful to keep the humorous and serious sections of *Joan of Arc* tightly compartmentalized. At the same time, Twain visualized himself as a scrupulously accurate historian. To someone who said that, in his article "St. Joan of Arc," Baudricourt should have been depicted as giving his own sword to Joan, Twain replied indignantly (in a letter never actually sent): "How do you know it was his 'own' sword? It could have been a borrowed one. I am cautious in matters of history, and you should not put statements in my mouth for which you cannot produce vouchers." This same man wanted Twain to say Joan's prophecies *in every case* came true instead of merely saying that she was the only person who had made such detailed prophecies and "scored fulfillment." To this criticism Twain answered: "I was particular not to claim that all her prophecies came true; for that would have been to claim that we have her whole list, whereas it is likely that she made some that failed and did not get upon the records. People do not recall prophecies that failed. Such is not the custom" (*36*, 182, 186–7). From his words, Twain appears to be the very model of the rational and conservative historian. While he was standing firm on a few small matters, however, he had capitulated on all the larger issues of Joan's life. Some kind of capitulation was almost inevitable given the impossible task of reconciling the prevalent nineteenth-century images of Joan of Arc and the Middle Ages. It remains for us to examine further why Twain's surrender was so complete and to determine the full relevance of this surrender to his conceptions of history.

Charles A. Beard has observed that "every piece of historical writing has been determined, in part at least, by the author's conception of the present and the future." [7] Clearly *Joan of Arc* is more a solution—or at least a reflection—of certain problems that were haunting Twain when he wrote it than it is a solution to the problem of Joan. The idea of progress, for example, is a distinct theme in the book; indeed, as Shaw noted, a theory of progress is implied in Twain's very prejudices. In despair as he was over the nineteenth century, Twain made little attempt to understand, let alone idealize, the fifteenth.[8] In the preface, furthermore, he suggests indirectly that moral standards have advanced from one century to another and that "judged by the standards of today, there is probably no illustrious character of four or five centuries ago whose

7. Bury, *The Idea of Progress,* introd., p. xxvii.

8. Mentor I. Williams, "Mark Twain's Joan of Arc," *Michigan Alumnus Quarterly Review,* 54 (1948), 243–50, argues that Twain, escaping from a business civilization, sought the "moral fiber, the ethical core of human society. He did not find it in the modern world. Like his contemporary, Henry Adams, he found it in the medieval world" (p. 250). There is, indeed, a basis of comparison with Adams, but Williams grossly oversimplifies it because in *Joan of Arc* there is as strong a hatred of medieval life—aside from its color and spectacle—as is found in any of Twain's work. I have attempted to demonstrate that Twain loved Joan because her personality and her ideals were so very different from those of the average human being of every age—but *especially* her own. If we must identify Twain's Joan with an historical epoch, Shaw's description of her as an "unimpeachable American school teacher in armor" is far more to the point (*Nine Plays,* p. 1006).

character could meet the test at all points" (*17*, xxi). Finally, at one point in the book, de Conte, in an episode reminiscent of *A Connecticut Yankee,* suddenly realizes that peasants are "people." Someday they will realize it too, he says, and "then I think they will rise up and demand to be regarded as part of the race, and that by consequence there will be trouble." De Conte adds that it is only "training" which keeps his contemporaries from realizing this fact (*18*, 65–6). Thus in moments of disgust with the Middle Ages, Twain cannot resist looking forward to his beloved French Revolution, even though it turns his narrator into almost as phenomenal a prophet as Joan herself. But such remarks as those he attributes to de Conte are more an instinctive reaction to an age he disliked (and which he never could bring himself to equate with his own except by implication) than the fruit of a firmly held conviction which we can genuinely label a belief in progress—as we can so easily label the Yankee's ideas. They constitute, indeed, a distinctly recessive theme in *Joan of Arc.* Even Twain's remarks on moral standards are introduced simply to suggest the uniqueness of Joan. Her character, he goes on to say, "can be measured by the standards of all times without misgiving or apprehension as to the result. Judged by any of them, judged by all of them, it is still flawless, it is still ideally perfect." In other words, the locus of values in *Joan of Arc* (and this constitutes the book's chief point of contrast with *A Connecticut Yankee*) lies not in an historical epoch, but in a personality who is clearly outside the logical processes of history. "It took six thousand years to produce her," says de Conte, "her like will not be seen on the earth again in fifty thousand" (*18*, 143).

It is not surprising that Twain groped for the miraculous during the 90's. Before *Joan of Arc* was published in 1895, the Paige typesetter had failed, the Charles L. Webster Co.

had gone into receivership in the general depression that was blanketing the country, and Twain had begun his exhausting round-the-world lecture tour in an effort to pay off his creditors. He had reached, moreover, what seemed to be an artistic and intellectual as well as a financial dead end. His belief in progress was hopelessly compromised by his resurgent pessimism and the growing fear of oligarchy that he expresses in *The American Claimant.* In addition, his already fading image of the idyllic village had finally disappeared in the moral dry rot of Dawson's Landing; his dream of Eden in the banalities of *Tom Sawyer Abroad, Adam's Diary,* and *Tom Sawyer Detective* and in the despair of old age and lost youth suggested by notes such as the one in which Twain imagined Huck as coming back "sixty years old, from nobody knows where—and crazy." He meets Tom again "and together they talk of old times, both are desolate, life has been a failure, all that was lovable is under the mold. They die together." [9] Clearly childhood memories and associations could no longer generate sustaining images. There was no refuge on the bosom of the river, no flight to the West, that could preserve the qualities of childhood from the ravages of life in time.

In the notebook which follows that in which Twain records the fate of Huck and Tom, however, there is the notation: "Chatto send me—Joan of Arc books." [1] He had decided to write what he himself realized would be "a companion piece to *The Prince and the Pauper*" (*32,* 960). His imagination turned from the defeated Huck and

9. Notebook 25 (1890–91), p. 24, published in *Notebook,* p. 212.

1. Notebook 26 (1891–92), p. 6. Twain's devotion to Joan was, of course, lifelong. His active interest in doing a biography of her, however, probably stems from the early 80's when he seems to have had a bibliography on the subject drawn up (see *32,* 958, and "Documents for 1892," DV 122, MTP). The impulse to write about her undergoes significant mutations in the 80's. One Notebook entry (21, 1885–87, p. 9), for example, reads: "Topics: The adventures of those runaway apprentices with the boy Jesus."

Tom to the dream of omnipotent innocence—to that other child masquerading as absolute ruler, who, like Tom Canty, had influenced history and yet was free from the taint of time and place. Joan brought to a brutal power struggle both an iron will that crushed all opposition and the goodness of childhood; for "she was a young girl . . . and her hero-heart was a young girl's heart too, with the pity and tenderness that are natural to it" (*17*, 239).

Unlike Edward and Tom, however, Joan transcends the very images with which she is associated. She is the Christ figure, the "ideally perfect" individual who "was not made as others are made" (*18*, 215),[2] the very incarnation of unfallen man—not a human but a superhuman child. During her trial and Passion, "she rose above the limitations and infirmities of our human nature" (*18*, 230). If history appeared to promise (as Satan was to demonstrate in *The Mysterious Stranger*) nothing except endless cycles of cruelty and slaughter by automatons, Twain could at least escape it emotionally and intuitively in the personality of Joan of Arc—the "intoxicated child." His phrase reveals the crux of Joan's significance for him. In her, his lifelong dream of Adamic innocence found a kind of religious sanction. Since she was, moreover, certified to be an authentic historical phenomenon by testimony taken "under oath" (as he naively boasted in his introduction) and the authority of legions of later writers including Michelet, Twain could worship her openly and at will and yet appease, by an appeal to the record, the voice of rationality within him.

Joan of Arc, nevertheless, is a deeply pessimistic book. If it is an affirmation of the existence and power of innocence, it is also a scathing record of its betrayal. While Edward magically puts everything to rights at the end of his

2. Ironically, ten years before Twain had written in Notebook 21 (1885–87), p. 46: "Who could endure a French Christ."

wanderings, while Huck (at least in *Huckleberry Finn*) succeeds in escaping to the West, Joan, on the other hand, is abandoned by her friends and burned by her enemies, and nothing de Conte and his creator are able to do can save her. The real ending of *Joan of Arc,* as we have already observed, is the scene at the stake, and de Conte's words on this occasion reinforce the theme of loss and failure that is central to the meaning of the book: "Yes she was gone from us: JOAN OF ARC! What little words they are, to tell of a rich world made empty and poor" (*18,* 282). Ultimately Joan remains only the bright dream of a bitter and disillusioned old man; her character and her fate, indeed, become a measure of the general depravity of the human race. "I believed these [reports that the King was going to ransom Joan]," de Conte notes late in life, "for I was young and had not yet found out the littleness and meanness of our poor human race, which brags about itself so much, and thinks it is better and higher than other animals" (*18,* 109). Only Joan's childhood companions—the other village children who followed her and formed her loyal and worshiping band—remain faithful to the end. Unlike the Huck of Twain's later fantasy, Joan manages to retain her sanity and her will but only at the cost of her freedom—the gift, significantly, not of civilization but of animistic natural forces—and her life.[3] Nor did her martyrdom have the kind of positive meaning for Twain that might have led to acceptance if not faith, as Melville accepts the similar fate of Billy Budd and Faulkner does that of the Corporal. The hollow rhetoric of Twain's superimposed "Conclusion" suggests his painful awareness that for him Joan's life and death promised neither the Re-

3. Twain describes Joan at one point as "born child of the sun, natural comrade of the birds, and all happy free creatures" (*18,* 124–5). For an extended discussion of Joan's relationship to nature and childish (prerational) sources of knowledge and power see Stone, pp. 15–18.

demption of man nor even the enduring reality of love and goodness but simply the rise of the hated French nation. It is, in fact, but one short step from *Joan of Arc* to *The Mysterious Stranger*—from a belief in the goodness, however meaningless ultimately, of one isolated individual to a belief in the corruptibility of all humanity, including specifically the young and the innocent.

"When a man's soul is starving, what does he care for meat and roof so he can but get that nobler hunger fed," remarks de Conte at one point in *Joan of Arc* when he is relating how the peasants flock in from miles around Vaucouleurs to see Joan (*17*, 91). The problem of belief here described is, of course, a favorite theme of modern literature. The solace from a world of blind forces that Mark Twain found in Joan, Henry Adams, for example—escaping from his own "scientific" theory of history, which promised nothing but social disintegration and world death—found in a strikingly similar fashion in the Virgin of the thirteenth century. She, too, represented an escape from remorseless causality: "Mary concentrated in herself the whole rebellion of man against fate: the whole protest against divine law; the whole contempt for human law as its outcome; the whole unutterable fury of human nature beating itself against the walls of its prison house, and suddenly seized by a hope that in the Virgin man had found a door of escape. She was above law." [4] As a recent critic of Adams has written: "He left *Chartres* as a wistful plea for that innocence, that intuition, which enables man to grasp some unity from life." [5] For both Twain and Adams faith in history was to lead only to a blind alley where bitterness and despair lay in wait. In his attempt to escape, Adams was scholar enough to build for himself an imposing ideal

4. *Mont-Saint-Michel and Chartres* (Boston and New York, Houghton Mifflin, 1933), pp. 273–4.

5. Jordy, *Henry Adams,* p. 283.

world in the thirteenth century. Ultimately, however, it was scarcely more stable than the modest dreams of Mark Twain, whose Huck grows up to madness and whose Joan is burnt without hope of resurrection.

9.

ESCAPE AS NIHILISM: *The Mysterious Stranger*

Again and again we pinned our hopes to some figure, but it always got drowned in the mud.

Selected Letters of Henry Adams

O but we dreamed to mend
What ever mischief seemed
To afflict mankind, but now
That winds of winter blow
Learn that we were crack-pated when we dreamed.

Yeats, "Nineteen Hundred and Nineteen"

When the relationship between man and the universe is one of disharmony and disequilibrium, we find that non-naturalistic, abstract styles are always produced . . . Instead of depicting natural appearances in all their overwhelming vitality, the will-to-art turns toward their spiritualization, towards the elimination of mass and corporeality, towards an approximation of the eternal tranquillity of other-worldly existence.

Joseph Frank, "Spatial Form in Modern Literature"

In his significant little book *Mark Twain at Work,* Bernard De Voto notes how Mark Twain's image of himself was impaired by the personal catastrophes of the 90's and goes on to describe the influence of this impairment on the form and themes of his later writing. "The gods had turned against their darling," says De Voto (p. 108). Twain's response to their betrayal was a sharper sense of personal guilt, which at the same time strengthened his conviction that *all* human nature was weak and fallible—indeed, hopelessly damned by corruption within and the iron chain of causality without. With his already meager belief in man thus further compromised, Twain's faith in civilization (the progress of man in society) could not long survive. By the early 1900's, in fact, pessimism regarding the "damned human race" had almost completely corroded away this faith.

In *Following the Equator* this corrosive process can most clearly be seen at work. During his trip around the world (1895–96), Twain's pessimism had found ready confirmation in the excesses of later nineteenth-century imperialism. He had abundant opportunity to contrast the values and actions of men of widely varying positions on the cultural scale. The resulting book was bitterly ironic; the ideal of civilization that Twain had so confidently held up in his early travel books, in *Following the Equator* is everywhere exposed as a sham and a delusion. The ideal, however, is exposed, as a whole, indirectly. The conception of progress still lingers on as the dominant image of social development, and no alternative theory of history is seriously proposed, though Twain is led to the very brink of a theory of recurrence. Certainly the faith which had, at least to some extent, animated the conception in his previous writings has disappeared.

Twain, for example, revisited Hawaii on his tour and presents in *Following the Equator* an account of the history of the Hawaiian kingdom roughly comparable to that which he had given much earlier in *Roughing It;* yet the pervasive irony of his comments in *Following the Equator* is not confined now to the religious customs of the missionaries and the pagan savage; it reveals that the historical record held a meaning for the old man far different from that which it had held for him in his youth. Kamehameha, writes Twain, "started the march of civilization" in 1792 when he "conceived the idea of enlarging his sphere of influence." This "courteous modern phrase," Twain goes on to explain, "means robbing your neighbor—for your neighbor's benefit; and the great theatre of its benevolences is Africa" (*20*, 27–9). Kamehameha defeated all opponents and began trading with the whites ("Savages are eager to learn from the white man any new way to kill each other, but it is not their habit to seize with avidity . . . the larger and nobler ideas which he offers them"). His son Liholiho tried to be a reformer ("A king has no proper business with reforming. His best policy is to keep things as they are; and if he can't do that, he ought to try to make them worse than they are") and destroyed the Established Church, an act which paved the way for missionaries (i.e. Protestantism), "business whites," and, eventually, republicanism. Had Kamehameha and Liholiho, then, put their benighted race on the road to perfection? Such, essentially, had been Twain's conclusion in 1867. The history of the Hawaiian kingdom, after all, was a kind of microcosm of the history of the West. Twain's interpretation of this history in 1896 reveals the full drift of his thought: "In Captain Cook's time (1778), the native population of the islands was estimated at 400,000 . . . it is today, per census, 25,000. All intelligent people praise Kamehameha I. and Liholiho for conferring upon the people the great boon of civilization. I would do it myself, but my intelligence is out of repair, now, from overwork" (*20*, 29–33).

Other passages in *Following the Equator* make Twain's specific objections to civilization even more apparent, though he seldom abandons his technique of heavy irony for any kind of direct assault. He has, for example, much to say regarding the traffic in Kanaka natives to work the

Queensland plantations. Why would they voluntarily leave their islands? Twain quotes a missionary pamphlet which says that the Kanakas want clothes, jewelry, and perfume and then goes on to comment: "For just one moment we have had a seeming flash of comprehension of the Kanaka's reason for exiling himself: he goes away to acquire *civilization.* Yes he was naked and not ashamed, now he is clothed and knows how to be ashamed; he was unenlightened, now he has a Waterbury watch; he was unrefined, now he has jewelry, and something to make him smell good; he was a nobody, a provincial, now he has been to far countries and can show off." But, continues Twain, even this "plausible" explanation is not as valid as it seems; the Kanaka goes home, loses or sells his gewgaws, and ends up with nothing but a newly learned ability to swear (*20,* 64–6). Such comments clearly reveal how observation of colonial practices increased Twain's awareness of the raw materialism of modern industrial civilization: its cash nexus, its false and pretentious values. He wrote the lesson he had learned in his notebook: "Money is the symbol of civilization; civilization is the root of all evil. Including war." [1] It is the falsity, pretentiousness, and hypocrisy of civilization that Twain attacks most vehemently in *Following the Equator.* Another of his gods had failed; *Following the Equator,* indeed, does to the progressivist dream what "Hadleyburg" had already done to the Jeffersonian ideal of the small town.

There is, perhaps, an even deeper note than disillusionment in the passage I have just quoted. Twain's words seem to echo faintly his dream of innocence—of freedom from the Moral Sense. The full drift of his thought is more fully revealed in a related notebook entry of the same period: "The first thing a missionary teaches a savage is indecency. He makes him put clothes on. He is as innocent & clean-

1. Notebook 32b(II) [1897–99], p. 63.

minded, up to that time as were our first parents when they walked naked before the lord & were not ashamed."[2] In Twain's work missionaries and clothing are persistent symbols of the Moral Sense and civilization (the shaper of the Moral Sense). We are reminded immediately, of course, of his later Adamic fantasies, which shed so much light on the meaning of *Huckleberry Finn.*[3] By the acquisition of clothes, in other words, the Kanaka native had repeated the fall of man.

Primitivism, however, is almost as foreign to the total theme of *Following the Equator* (if such a discursive series of impressions, anecdotes, and experiences can be said to have a theme) as the idea of progress. Man may have degenerated—at least in the sense of having gone from bad to worse as his capability of doing evil increased—but the main point emphasized by the book is his eternal corruption. There is, therefore, much sympathy for native populations in *Following the Equator* but little idealization. The Australian aborigines, for example, before the coming of the white man "diligently and deliberately kept population down by infanticide—largely; but mainly by certain other methods. He did not need to practice these artificialities any more after the white man came. The white man knew ways of keeping down population which were worth several of his." Twain goes on to describe a case in which the whites had used poison on the natives. He notes that poison was merciful and quick compared to other methods of extermination used and then adds: "There are many humorous things in the world; among them the white man's notion that he is less savage than other savages" (*20,* 185–92). This idea is even more succinctly expressed in a late notebook: "Difference bet. sav-

2. Notebook 32a(I), p. 16. See also 32b(I), p. 28: "What is civilization? Clothes. What is back of all vast political powers (thrones, Popedoms etc.) [?] Clothes.

3. See above, pp. 142–4.

age & civilized man, one is painted, the other gilded." [4]

In short, Twain could not embrace primitivism after he had denied the value of civilization simply because he could no longer believe in the innocence of any mortal individual. Indeed, he had become obsessed with the problem of innate evil. Noting that an Indian Thug had once compared his own love of hunting men with the English passion for animal hunting, Twain commented: "That must really be the secret of the rise and development of Thuggee. The joy of killing! The joy of seeing killing done—these are traits of the human race at large. We white people are merely modified Thugs; Thugs fretting under the restraints of a not very thick skin of civilization; Thugs who long ago enjoyed the slaughter of the Roman arena, and later the burning of doubtful Christians in the public squares, and who now, with the Thugs of Spain and Nîmes, flock to enjoy the blood and misery of the bull-ring" (*21*, 112). This passage is a late and grim echo of his comments in *The Innocents Abroad* and *Roughing It* on the "instinctive" joy man receives from camping out.[5]

Theoretically, of course, there was no place for innate qualities (good or bad) in Twain's philosophical system. His "moral sense," like that of David Hartley in the eighteenth century, was based ultimately on the Lockean *tabula rasa,* although as a post-Darwinian he was careful to give at least lip service to the idea of heredity. For Twain and the whole sensationalist school, evil was supposedly the result of socially undesirable associations—themselves the product of faulty training.[6] Neither Twain nor his intellectual forbears, however, were ever really able to legislate human nature out of existence. We have re-

4. 36 (1903), p. 34.

5. See above, pp. 57–8.

6. See "What Is Man?" and Sampson, *Progress in the Age of Reason,* pp. 43–66.

peatedly observed that it is a persistent theme in Twain's writing: whether used to explain Huck's goodness (his "sound heart") or used (more commonly) to explain the prevalence and persistence of human greed, cowardice, and cruelty. The mob images found in so many of his books are his attempt to make vivid this hard, unmalleable core of human nature which is at the heart of any culture. His extremely pessimistic conception of history as an endless empty change springs from a growing sense of evil inherent in man. On the other hand, his conceptions of history as progressive development or as a process of development and decline were responses to his theory of the Moral Sense.

Actually, in *Following the Equator* Twain has not completely abandoned the idea of progress. To his comments on the Thugs, for instance, he adds a significant qualification: "Still [i.e. although we love to kill], we have made some progress—microscopic, and in truth scarcely worth mentioning, and certainly nothing to be proud of—still, it is progress: we no longer take pleasure in slaughtering or burning helpless men. We have reached a little altitude where we may look down upon the Indian Thugs with a complacent shudder; and we may even hope for a day, many centuries hence, when our posterity will look down upon us in the same way" (*21*, 125–6). The vast moral disparity between the worlds of Arthur and the Yankee has here been reduced to a "microscopic" quantity. This passage, nevertheless, is perhaps the most optimistic in the entire book. For more extravagant claims Twain had only scorn. During his discussion of the Kanakas, he ridiculed an English minister who had described how the "tide of civilization" was rolling on into Asia "humanizing, not destroying" and who had invoked Campbell's couplet, "Come, bright Improvement! on the car of Time, / And rule the spacious world from clime to clime." To such sentiments, Twain had a devastating rejoinder: "Very well, Bright Improvement has arrived . . . with her civilization, and her Waterbury watch, and her umbrella, and her third-quality profanity, and her humanizing-not-destroying machinery, and her hundred-and-eighty-death-rate [per thousand among Kanaka laborers], and everything is going along just as handsome!" (*20,* 69–70).

Twain's lingering hopefulness was in part residual and indicative of his undying hatred of "feudalism," in part a response to his increasingly pro-British sentiments during the 90's. This hopefulness is evident also in another passage in which he endorses imperialism:

> The sins of the times show plainly enough what is going to happen. All the savage lands in the world are going to be brought under subjection to the Christian governments of Europe. I am not sorry, but glad. This coming fate might have been a calamity to those savage peoples two hundred years ago; but now it will in some cases be a benefaction. The sooner the seizure is consummated the better for the savages. The dreary and dragging ages of bloodshed and disorder and oppression will give place to peace and order, and the reign of law. When one considers what India was under the Hindoo and Mohammed Rulers, and what she is now . . . he must concede that the most fortunate thing that has ever befallen that empire was the establishment of British supremacy there. The savage lands of the world are to pass to alien possession, their peoples to the mercies of alien rulers. Let us hope and believe they will all benefit by the change.
>
> [*21,* 300–1]

This passage also indicates Twain's rejection, on the whole, of any kind of easy primitivism. If men are innately evil, he seems to be saying, the rule of law possesses at least the negative value of keeping them from indiscriminate slaughter. On the other hand, he notes elsewhere that modern civilization had increased the efficiency and the availability of tools of slaughter. This intellectual dilemma, commonplace enough for the twentieth-century mind, illustrates how the self-evident assumption of Twain's youth—that history demonstrated progress—had become the complex riddle of his old age.

Far more characteristic of *Following the Equator* than qualified hopes is Twain's growing conviction that history was empty of *any* redemptive value. In an extraordinary passage, which looks far ahead into the twentieth century, he describes the fascination of India, with its "monotony of dust-colored dead levels and scattering bunches of trees and mud villages. It is not a beautiful country, yet there is an enchantment about it." The cause of the spell cast by India, Twain goes on to say, is history. "It is that that affects you, a haunting sense of the myriads of human lives that have blossomed, and withered, and perished here, repeating and repeating, century after century, and age after age, the barren and meaningless process; it is this sense that gives to this forlorn, uncomely land power to speak to the spirit and make friends with it; to speak to it with a voice bitter with satire, but eloquent with melancholy" (*21*, 129). The touches of romantic rhetoric in this passage (even more in evidence further on when Twain talks about "man and his vanities") should not blind us to the significance of its main contention: that history is a "barren and meaningless process"—change that is no change, recurrence without purpose.

Because his gaze was fixed so intently at this time on the supposed immutability of human nature, Twain had thus reached a position far more drastic even than that of Henry and Brooks Adams, whose theories of decline were really a long lamentation for the values of a political

Golden Age in the past.[7] In his comment on India, Twain, for all his rhetoric, was much closer in spirit to Eliot's Thomas Becket, who ironically describes the past as "not worth forgetting" and who does

> . . . not know very much of the future
> Except that from generation to generation
> The same things happen again and again.
> Men learn little from others' experience.[8]

For Becket, as for his creator, history is without teleological significance because of the radically defective nature of man. This essentially is the conception of history (implied in *Huckleberry Finn*) which Twain was working toward in *Following the Equator* and which he was to develop explicitly at some length in *The Mysterious Stranger*. But Eliot's vision is Christian and apocalyptic; although we must start with temporal, ever-changing experience, we come to see its dependence upon the timeless—"Only through time time is conquered." [9] For Twain, on the other hand, those very forces which were pressing on him an agonizing awareness of the world of flux, were, at the

7. Theoretically, Brooks Adams' "law" was cyclical: i.e. any society moved from an imaginative, agrarian, decentralized stage to one which was intellectual, materialistic, and centralized. The latter eventually brought about its own disintegration through sterility, and presumably the whole process would be repeated again. Yet Adams' *Law of Civilization and Decay* ends ominously. We are more materialistic than the Romans ("the Romans were never wholly sordid, nor did they ever niggle") and "we lack the stream of barbarian blood which made the Middle Ages" (New York, Vintage, 1955, p. 308). Clearly what Brooks, like Henry, was interested in stressing was the long (and probably irreversible) decline from the Middle Ages. Written during the free silver controversy, his book is a curious commingling of the Jeffersonian-Agrarian tradition with the romantic medievalism of Ruskin.

8. *Murder in the Cathedral* (New York, Harcourt, Brace, 1935), p. 24.

9. T. S. Eliot, *Four Quartets* (New York, Harcourt, Brace, 1943), p. 5. My comment on Eliot's conception of time is a close paraphrase of Morris Weitz, "T. S. Eliot: Time as a Mode of Salvation," *Sewanee Review, 60* (1952), 58–9.

same time and by their very nature, destroying the imaginative and spiritual validity of his own center of the turning wheel. Indeed, it is this dilemma which presented itself to him when he sat down to write *The Mysterious Stranger.*

"Would you like to see a history of the progress of the human race?—its development of that product which it calls civilization?" Satan asks his young companions in *The Mysterious Stranger.* Upon their affirmative answer, he presents a vision of Cain murdering Abel, followed by an endless vista of wars, murders, and massacres—Hebrew, Egyptian, Greek, Roman, and those of the "ages of Europe." "It is a remarkable progress," he adds:

> In five or six thousand years five or six high civilizations have risen, flourished, commanded the wonder of the world, then faded out and disappeared, and not one of them except the latest ever invented any sweeping and adequate way to kill people. They all did their best—to kill being the chiefest ambition of the human race and the earliest incident in its history—but only the Christian civilization has scored a triumph to be proud of. Two or three centuries from now it will be recognized that all the competent killers are Christians; then the pagan world will go to school to the Christian—not to acquire his religion, but his guns. [27, 108–11]

Satan goes on to portray the future explicitly for the boys: "before our eyes nation after nation drifted by, during two or three centuries, a mighty procession, raging, struggling, wallowing through seas of blood, smothered in battle smoke . . . and always we heard the thunder of the guns and the cries of the dying." The ultimate cause of the endless cycle of slaughter, he concludes, finally, is human nature: the usurpations of minorities; the acquiescence of the majority.

"The first man was a hypocrite and a coward, qualities which have not yet failed in his line; it is the foundation upon which all civilizations have been built" (27, 111–12).

Here human corruption is envisaged as a quality inherent in Adam; no fall is involved. Corruption, in other words, is not the result of but anterior to civilization—the First Cause of all social forms. Elsewhere in the book, corruption and the historical evils resulting from corruption are blamed on the Moral Sense; man does wrong because of false notions of right and wrong inevitably inculcated by society. The torture of a heretic, for example, is compared to the exploitation of factory workers by "rich and very holy" proprietors, who "pay to these poor brothers and sisters of theirs . . . only enough to keep them from dropping dead with hunger." Significantly, in this passage Twain directly attacks the technology he had so long celebrated and actually goes on to argue that the factory system is even *worse* than medieval torture: "They broke him [the tortured man] on the wheel and smashed him to rags and pulp after we left [says Satan], and he is dead now and free of your precious race, but these poor slaves here [the factory workers]—why they have been dying for years and some of them will not escape from life for years to come" (27, 50–3).

Such is the conception of human history in *The Mysterious Stranger*—a conception that contributes heavily to the total pessimism of the book. It is, however, only one aspect of this pessimism, just as Twain's belief in progress in the 1880's was only part of his vision of human experience during that period. What of his dream of escape from history—his complex image of goodness, stasis, freedom that had coalesced in the figure of the boy floating down the Mississippi on a raft? Clearly, in *The Mysterious Stranger* as in *Following the Equator,* a coherent primitivism was impossible for Twain because of his overwhelming sense of the evil inherent in man. As Gladys Bellamy has noted, "he can no longer depend upon his boys for the saving grace." [1] Nikolaus and Seppi and Theodor in *The Mysterious Stranger* have more pity than their elders but they are just as cowardly. On one occasion, for example, the boys want to warn Marget and Ursula that the community suspects them of witchcraft, but, as Theodor admits: "we backed down when it came to the pinch, being afraid. We found that we were not manly enough to do a generous action when there was a chance that it would get us into trouble" (27, 59–66). On another occasion Theodor stones a woman being hanged because if he "had not done as the others did it would have been noticed and spoken of." In his heart he is sorry for her, but "all were throwing stones and each was watching his neighbor" (27, 114–15). To be sure, Theodor leaves one witch-burning because "it was too dreadful," and at another he gives the victim an apple (27, 60); but these gestures remain his nearest approach to independent moral action. In such scenes Twain preserves the situation so common in his writing of the cruel mob observed by a boy who either pities and (if possible) aids the victim or is himself the victim. The sole—though crucial—difference in *The Mysterious Stranger* is the shift in the moral stance of the boy: pity has been rendered impotent by fear.

Unfallen, free from the Moral Sense, master of "time and distance" (27, 26, 114), Satan is the one explicitly Adamic figure in the book. His "innocence," however, leads not so much to goodness as to indifference—indeed, to what, at least to mortal eyes, seems very close to callousness. If nothing else, his name and the curious fact that he is nephew to the great fallen angel would suggest Twain's deeply ambivalent feelings toward him. Time was

1. *Mark Twain as a Literary Artist* (Norman, Univ. of Oklahoma Press, 1950), p. 361.

cruel, but eternity was insensate and capricious.[2] Only in animals could Twain still locate innate goodness, and they merely served to illuminate more sharply the horror of man. A dog, for example, who tries to save the life of the master who has misused him, exhibits the same enduring and instinctive loyalty and sense of responsibility that Twain in other books had associated with Edward, Huck, and Jim (27, 54–7).

Yet as the paths of escape narrowed for Twain, the need increased. "Raft" imagery keeps reappearing in his writing of the 90's. "If I had my way I would sail on forever and never go to live on the solid ground again," he remarks in *Following the Equator* (*21*, 290–1). Stasis predicated on physical isolation, however, was inadequate for obvious reasons; even Huck and Jim's paradise had been invaded by the Duke and the Dauphin—those grotesque symbols of the very civilization from which the boy and the Negro were attempting to flee. By 1890, for Twain as for the rest of the country, the frontier was closed; in the years ahead, symbolic as well as literal escape to the wilderness would become increasingly difficult. Social stasis was an equally futile hope. On the first page of *The Mysterious Stranger,* Austria in 1390 is described as "far away from the world, and asleep." The boy narrator goes on to note that Eseldorf, his village, was "in the middle of that sleep, being in the middle of Austria. It drowsed in peace in the deep privacy of a hilly and woodsy solitude where news from the world hardly ever came to disturb its dreams, and was infinitely content." Here Twain instinctively (not, I think, ironically) evokes the Jeffersonian idyl, but, of course, its validity is contradicted by the whole drift of the story—even by the

2. Twain's ambivalent feelings toward the Deity in *The Mysterious Stranger* have been aptly compared with those of Hardy by Edwin S. Fussel, "The Structural Problem of 'The Mysterious Stranger'," *Studies in Philology, 49* (1952), 97.

very name of the village. It is significant that, in reworking his story, he transferred it from Hannibal, as if the lingering associations of Hannibal prevented him from giving free vent to his nihilism. Certain medieval practices, moreover, always remained his ultimate images of inhumanity. In his "Eddypus" manuscript Twain carefully makes the distinction between a "dully dozing" southern village and its medieval counterpart; even with slavery, he says, the southern village had no Inquisition and no burning of heretics (p. 29). Death by fire (which figures prominently in *The Mysterious Stranger*) has an important psychological meaning for Twain. It is clearly related to his feelings of guilt about his brother Henry, who perished in a steamboat tragedy, as well as those about the drunk who burned up in jail because Twain had given him matches.[3]

In the face of such terrible visions, escape was conceivable only on far more drastic terms: nothing less than severance of the direct relationship between the mind and the world. It was, indeed, impossible unless one or the other were totally destroyed. Thus insanity was a possible means of escape. "Are you so unobservant as not to have found out that sanity and happiness are an impossible combination?" asks Satan after he has made the kindly Father Peter insane. "No sane man can be happy, for to him life is real and he sees what a fearful thing it is. Only the mad can be happy." Death, naturally, was equally effective. The narrator says of Satan with more truth than he is aware of at the time: "He didn't seem to know any way to do a person a favor except by killing him or making a lunatic out of him" (27, 130–1). The alternative to death and insanity was to destroy the world while leaving the mind intact; and this Twain tried to do by means of a curious extension of the dream image—his image of "un-

3. Dixon Wecter makes this point in *Sam Clemens of Hannibal* (Boston, 1952), pp. 253–6.

reality." According to Bellamy, "the urge toward escapism enlarges the dream motif until the dream finally engulfs the whole of life, the ugliness as well as the beauty."[4] "Nothing exists but you," says Satan to Theodor. "And you are but a thought—a vagrant thought, a useless thought, a homeless thought, wandering forlorn among the empty eternities" (27, 140). In his desire to escape the shock and disillusionment of life in time, Twain had arrived close to the modern existentialist position.

Such a solution to life's problems may have had an immense therapeutic value for Twain; it may, indeed, as De Voto has suggested, have brought him back from the brink of insanity.[5] As an artistic device, however, it is less successful. Twain makes his escape by fiat not by art, because his image of escape had been destroyed in the process of its transformation and he had nothing concrete to substitute for it. A literary image is a complex of sensuous, compelling, and value-laden associations. In *Huckleberry Finn,* Twain's image of escape is compounded of the naive innocence of childhood, the godlike stature of the raftsmen, and the sense of release (with its possibility of moral freedom) and stasis attendant on sleep, drifting, and physical isolation from society. His image is "unreal" only in the sense that it describes a reality transcending the flux of empirically centered experience—a source of values beyond the reach of life in time and history though constantly in conflict with it.

In *The Mysterious Stranger* the components of this complex image are systematically rejected as themselves being without value. The "unreality" of the dream concept is retained but this "unreality" now is not the unreality of transcendence mirrored in concrete images but the unreality of total negation; the dream, in other words, has

4. *Mark Twain as a Literary Artist,* p. 360.
5. *Mark Twain at Work,* pp. 129–30.

become a device for exorcism rather than artistic creation. The sole remaining "reality" is the existential "I," but Twain makes no serious attempt to conceive of this "I" imagistically as certain twentieth-century writers have done. It is, moreover, even debatable whether the ending of *The Mysterious Stranger* works out in intellectual terms. Edwin Fussell has attempted to show how Twain prepares for the ending through various "levels of dreaming" in the book, but he as much as admits that to take the ending at its face value is to turn the rest of the book into an epistemological nightmare.[6]

But if Twain fails to develop a coherent imaginative response to what Camus has called the "absurdity" of life, he succeeds, nevertheless, at the more modest level in making this absurdity vivid, albeit in nineteenth-century terms. The real theme of *The Mysterious Stranger*—the theme which, as it is developed concretely, gives to the book its enduring value—is not the literal unreality but the meaninglessness of life. Life is insubstantial only in its futility, its lack of stable and enduring values; only in the face of the indifference (if not the malice) of God, the weakness and the limited vision of man, the sense of the monotony and repetition of human events. Camus' "absurdity" is Twain's "vanity," a note sounded again and again in the book. Satan's laughter reaches out to embrace all human pretensions. On one such occasion Theodor recounts how Satan suddenly sobers up a little and says: "But, after all, it is not all ridiculous [i.e. man's pride in his deeds]; there is a sort of pathos about it when one remembers how few are your days, how childish your pomps, and what shadows you are" (27, 53). To the extent that men were "shadows" —without the dignity of enduring substance and final ends —they were "unreal." But this is, of course, a far cry from solipsism.

6. Fussel, pp. 95–104.

What is the meaning of history, asks Satan rhetorically in *The Mysterious Stranger*? What does the endless, empty cycle of civilizations amount to? He answers his own question by remarking that it amounts to "nothing at all." "You gain nothing," he explains; "you always come out where you went in. For a million years the race has gone on monotonously propagating itself . . . to what end? No wisdom can guess" (27, 111–12). Twain leaves the problem of an adequate conception of history—of visible images of the past, present, and future or viable images of the transcendence of time—at exactly the point at which the contemporary artist has been forced to construct new hypotheses and new artistic forms in accord with these hypotheses. Driven by a similar impulse to recover an order and stasis beyond time or simply to portray the sterility of a time-ridden world, certain modern writers have abandoned naturalism for deliberate anachronism, isolated image groups (i.e. the blurring or complete denial of narrative and even syntactical sequence), extravagant use of myth, symbolic characterization, and stream-of-consciousness techniques—all of which tend to work against the normal, chronological structure of the literary medium. For these writers, as Joseph Frank has noted, the mythical imagination has supplanted the objective historical imagination.[7] Twain's work can be most fruitfully viewed as a significant step down the long road to this transformation. In *The Mysterious Stranger,* the movement away from a naturalistic style is obvious and explicit.

At the same time, the relative success of the modern writer in meeting the imaginative challenge occasioned by the failure of history throws a good deal of light on certain of the root causes of Twain's artistic imperfections: on the one hand, a frequent failure to bring his deepest vision

7. Pages 379–92. My comments in this paragraph draw heavily on Frank's excellent article.

into focus or even to acknowledge it completely (e.g. *A Connecticut Yankee* and *The Prince and the Pauper*); on the other, the unfulfilled attempt to wed vision to substantial form (e.g. *Joan of Arc* and *The Mysterious Stranger*). Even in *Huckleberry Finn,* although Twain succeeded brilliantly in suggesting a mode of being apart from history, he was still a slave to the time-sequential structure of his naturalistic narrative and the logical demands of a "social problem" plot. However long he allowed Huck and Jim to loaf on Jackson's Island or to float on the bosom of the river, Twain was committed to taking them somewhere else; they could not forever drift downstream, least of all into the deep South. Here, indeed, is the core of Twain's dilemma in the book and the reason why the final chapters seem such a drastic falling off from the central episodes.

The fact is that Huck cannot be meaningfully separated from his river surroundings *because* his largest dimension is mythological. For the mythological imagination "place, not time . . . [is] the crucial form of perception . . . For mythical thinking the relation between what a thing 'is' and the place where it is situated is never purely external and accidental; the place is itself a part of the thing's being, and the place confers very special ties upon the thing." [8] It is "place" in this sense which gives Huck his real significance, yet it is place which Twain is eventually forced to violate because of the growing absurdity of the plot after the raft has passed Cairo. That he hesitated so long to remove Huck from the river suggests Twain's intuitive awareness that Huck would lose stature and meaning were he to be separated from the images which define him—indeed, which are an integral part of his being. The best that can

8. Isabel G. MacCaffrey, *Paradise Lost as "Myth"* (Cambridge, Harvard Univ. Press, 1959), pp. 69–70, and n. 25. The quotation dealing with mythical thinking is taken by MacCaffrey from Ernst Cassirer, *Mythical Thought,* trans. Ralph Manheim (New Haven, Yale Univ. Press, 1955), p. 92.

be said of the final scenes is that they are a grotesque and heavy-handed parody of the true romance of the river. But Huck's loss of stature—his sudden descent from mythical hero to little boy—is jarring, disorienting, and anti-climactic. A complete victim of the plot, he is only freed from its effects when Twain arbitrarily dissolves it by announcing that Jim has been emancipated all along. Then and only then can Huck return to his appropriate place. Or can he? His plan "to light out for the Territory ahead of the rest" (*13*, 405) betrays its weakness in its very phraseology, for it acknowledges that the "sivilizing" Aunt Sallys will always be close behind. Huck's place, in other words, was too geographical, too localized; it was threatened by both the chronological demands of the conventional novel and the larger chronology of history. Thus the image of the river was productive of one great book but of no enduring vision, point of view, or style because it was everywhere vulnerable to the very time it sought to transcend. Tormented by history, which for most of his life he alternately sought to embrace and cast away, Twain was finally driven in *The Mysterious Stranger* to a passionate, frantic, arbitrary denial of its power to hurt him: "It is all a dream—a grotesque and foolish dream" (*27*, 140). For the Twain of *The Mysterious Stranger,* as for so many later writers, history (to paraphrase Stephen Dedalus) had become a nightmare from which one must—somehow—awake to live and write.

INDEX

YALE STUDIES IN ENGLISH

This volume is the one hundred and fiftieth of the Yale Studies in English, founded by Albert Stanburrough Cook in 1898 and edited by him until his death in 1927. Tucker Brooke succeeded him as editor, and served until 1941, when Benjamin C. Nangle succeeded him.

The following volumes are still in print. Orders should be addressed to YALE UNIVERSITY PRESS, New Haven, Connecticut.

87. OSBORN, L. B. The Life, Letters, and Writings of John Hoskyns. $3.50.
92. RICH, T. Harington and Ariosto: A Study in Elizabethan Verse Translation. $2.00.
102. WORTHINGTON, JANE. Wordsworth's Reading of Roman Prose. $2.50.
109. BORST, WILLIAM A. Lord Byron's First Pilgrimage. $3.75.
110. MICHEL, LAURENCE (editor). *The Tragedy of Philotas.* By Samuel Daniel. $3.75.
112. CALDER, GRACE J. The Writing of *Past and Present.* A Study of Carlyle's Manuscripts. $3.75.
113. DONALDSON, E. TALBOT. *Piers Plowman:* The C-Text and Its Poet. $5.00.
114. LYON, JUDSON STANLEY. *The Excursion.* A Study. $4.00.
116. SEYBOLD, ETHEL. Thoreau: The Quest and the Classics. $3.00.
117. KNIGHT, DOUGLAS. Pope and the Heroic Tradition. A Critical Study of His *Iliad.* $3.00.
119. DAVIS, MERRELL R. Melville's *Mardi.* A Chartless Voyage. $4.00.
120. WAITH, EUGENE M. The Pattern of Tragicomedy in Beaumont and Fletcher. $4.00.
124. QUIRK, RANDOLPH. The Concessive Relation in Old English Poetry. $4.00.

125. MARTZ, L. L. The Poetry of Meditation. $5.00.
126. HOLDEN, WILLIAM P. Anti-Puritan Satire, 1572–1642. $3.75.
129. BRADLEY, JOHN LEWIS. Ruskin's Letters from Venice, 1851–1852. $5.00.
130. LEYBURN, ELLEN DOUGLASS. Satiric Allegory: Mirror of Man. $3.00.
131. LORD, GEORGE DE FOREST. Homeric Renaissance. The *Odyssey* of George Chapman. $3.00.
132. BOWDEN, EDWIN T. The Themes of Henry James. $3.00.
134. SCHUTTE, WILLIAM M. Joyce and Shakespeare: A Study in the Meaning of *Ulysses*. $4.00.
135. UNDERWOOD, DALE. Etherege and the Seventeenth-Century Comedy of Manners. $4.00.
136. FRANK, R. W., JR. *Piers Plowman* and the Scheme of Salvation. $4.00.
137. BERGER, H., JR. The Allegorical Temper. Vision and Reality in Book II of Spenser's *Faerie Queene*. $5.00.
138. YOUNG, RICHARD B., FURNISS, W. TODD, MADSEN, WILLIAM G. Three Studies in the Renaissance: Sidney, Jonson, Milton. $5.00.
139. HOWES, ALAN B. Yorick and the Critics. Sterne's Reputation in England, 1760–1868. $4.50.
141. BLOOM, HAROLD. Shelley's Mythmaking. $5.00.
142. KERNAN, ALVIN. The Cankered Muse. Satire of the English Renaissance. $5.00.
143. PAULSON, RONALD. Theme and Structure in Swift's *Tale of a Tub*. $5.00.
144. RIDENOUR, GEORGE M. The Style of *Don Juan*. $4.00.
145. HIRSCH, E. D., JR. Wordsworth and Schelling. $5.00.
146. SPENCER, CHRISTOPHER. Davenant's *Macbeth*. $5.00.
147. LYNEN, JOHN F. The Pastoral Art of Robert Frost. $4.50.
148. TOWNSEND, J. BENJAMIN. John Davidson, Poet of Armageddon. $7.50.
149. KNAPP, MARY E. Prologues and Epilogues of the Eighteenth Century. $6.00.
150. SALOMON, ROGER B. Twain and the Image of History. $5.00.
151. BOULGER, JAMES D. Coleridge as Religious Thinker. $5.00.